WALKS WITH WRITERS

Walks With Writers

New literary walks in **Old Berkshire**

Elizabeth Cader-Cuff

First published in 1999 by
E. Cuff
Tel: 0118 988 2674

© 1999 Elizabeth Cader-Cuff

All rights reserved. No part of this publication may be reproduced or transmitted in any form or by any means, electronic or mechanical, including photocopy, recording, or any information storage and retrieval system, without permission in writing from the publisher.

British Library Cataloguing-in-Publication Data
A catalogue record for this book is available from the British Library.

ISBN 0 9535695 0 0

Illustrations by the author.

Edited and designed by
D & N Publishing
Membury Business Park, Lambourn Woodlands, Hungerford, Berkshire.

Colour scanning by Microset Imaging Limited, Witney, Oxfordshire.

Printed and bound by Times Offset (M) Sdn Bhd.

Author's Acknowledgements

My thanks are given to fellow members of the local groups of the Ramblers' Association for help in trying out the walks and general information-gathering. Also to the staff of the Local Studies Section of Berkshire County Libraries, particularly the Reading branch.

The illustrations show houses and other places associated with the writers as they appear today.
PLEASE RESPECT THE PRIVACY OF PRESENT RESIDENTS.

CONTENTS

Map of Old Berkshire, Showing Location of the Walks 6
Preface 7

Setting the Scene 8
WALK 1   A Windsor Great Park walk of five and a half miles, taking in some places known to Alexander Pope, Samuel Pepys and other writers   10

Alexander Pope, 1688–1744 13
WALK 2   A short walk of about a mile, circling the Binfield home of Alexander Pope   18

Jane Austen, 1775–1817 20
WALK 3   A Jane Austen walk of six miles, starting from Kintbury, which refers also to Richard Adams and Robert Harris   25

Mary Russell Mitford, 1787–1855 27
WALK 4   A Mary Russell Mitford walk of eight miles, from Three Mile Cross   33

Thomas Hughes, 1822–1896 34
WALK 5   A Thomas Hughes walk of nine miles from Uffington, which refers also to John Betjeman and Walter Scott   40

Robert Bridges, 1844–1930 42
WALK 6   A Robert Bridges walk of four and a half miles from Yattendon   47

Oscar Wilde, 1854–1900 49
WALK 7   An Oscar Wilde walk of two miles in Central Reading, which refers also to Jane Austen and Kenneth Grahame   54

Kenneth Grahame, 1859–1932 56
WALK 8   A Kenneth Grahame walk of three and a half miles from Cookham Dean   63
WALK 9   A Kenneth Grahame walk of five miles from Pangbourne, which also passes places linked with Lytton Strachey, DH Lawrence and Jerome K Jerome   64

Jerome Klapka Jerome, 1859–1927 66
WALK 10   A Jerome K Jerome walk of four miles from Sonning, which refers also to Jane Austen   71

Laurence Binyon, 1869–1943 72
WALK 11   A Laurence Binyon walk of four and a half miles to the Ridgeway and Aldworth, or one of three miles to Aldworth   75

John Masefield, 1878–1967 77
Agatha Christie, 1890–1976 80
WALK 12   A John Masefield walk of five miles from Aston Tirrold, which also visits the grave of Agatha Christie   81

Edward Thomas, 1878–1917 83
WALK 13   An Edward Thomas walk of almost ten miles, along some of the Icknield Way and the Ridgeway   85

David Herbert Lawrence, 1885–1930 87
WALK 14   A DH Lawrence walk of five and a half miles in and around Hermitage   91

John Betjeman, 1906–1984 93
WALK 15   A John Betjeman walk of six or seven miles from Farnborough in Berkshire   98

More Writers of Town and Country 100

Visiting Writers to Ridgeway and River 105
WALK 16   A five-mile walk in Thomas Hardy's North Wessex, which also passes where Dean Swift stayed in 1714   109

Acknowledgements 112

O X F O R D
Shilton Part of Berkshire
Longford
Wolvercot
Port Mead
OXFORD
Charwell Riv.
From Burford
From Bampton
to Gloocester by Cirencester
Whiteham
Cumnor
Hinksey
Kenington
Sunningwell
Radley
ABINGDON
Isis River
LEECHLADE
Eaton
Buckland
Longworth
Fifield
Kingston Bagpuze
Frilford
Marcham
FARRINGDON
HIGH WORTH
Coleshill
Great Coxwell
Shrivenham
Stanford
Hartford
Pusey
Charney Basset
East Hanny
Drayton
Steventon
Milton
Sutton
Clifton
Little Wittenham
Long Wittenham
DORC
Longcot
Uffington
Kingston Lisle
Childrey
Denchworth
Charlow
Ardington
Harwell
Didcot
Brightwell
WALL
Compton
White Horse
WANTAGE
Letcomb Regis
Locking
E. Hendred
W. Hendred
Chilton
Blewbury
Upton
Cholsey
Ashbury
Ashdown Park
Letcomb Basset
Letcomb Downs
Great Fawley
Farnborough
EAST ILSLEY
Blewbury Down
Moulsford
High Down
Streatley
Aldworth
Lamborn Down
Lit. Fawley
LAMBORN
From Marlborough
from Marlborough
Chaddleworth
Catmore
Compton
Peasmore
Hampstead Norris
Ashampstead
East Garston
Great Shefford
Little Shefford
Leckhampstead
Chively
Oare
Evington
Welford
Winterborn
Boxford
Frilsham
Bucklebury
County Cross
Chilton
Wickham Chapel
HUNGERFORD
Bath & Bristol Road
Speen
Shaw
Newbury
Thatcham
Midgham
Beenham
Woolhampton
Kintbury
Hampstead Marshal
Enborne
Brimpton
Inkpen
Shalborne
West Woodhay
Newtown
Wasing
Ham
Buttermeer
Salisbury Road
to Andover
to Winchester
to Chichester
H A M P S H I R E
W I L T S H I R E

PREFACE

This book celebrates the work and lives of writers who have lived in or been closely associated with Berkshire. 'Old Berkshire' refers to the county as it was known by most of these writers, who lived before the boundary changes of 1974. Wider stretches of fine walking country, encompassing downland, rivers and woods, can thus be included, although they are now in Oxfordshire.

Sixteen walks are outlined, with route directions and maps, in areas the writers knew and described. These will show why many creative writers chose to settle in the Royal County, and how it enhanced their work. Changes have, of course, occurred over the years, and will continue to do so, but the poems, plays and novels featured in this book have conveyed the beauty of the local scenery and helped to preserve it; if we remember these writers, and continue to walk in their footsteps, we will help to protect a heritage of literature and landscape few countries enjoy.

All walks are covered by Sheets 174 or 175 of the Ordnance Survey Landranger Series, or the corresponding OS Pathfinder and Explorer maps, which give more detail. Some walks can be reached by public transport. A bus service has run to the Ridgeway for some years, for instance; details can be obtained from Local Authority Transport Services. Cars, if needed, can be parked where 'Start' is indicated on the maps.

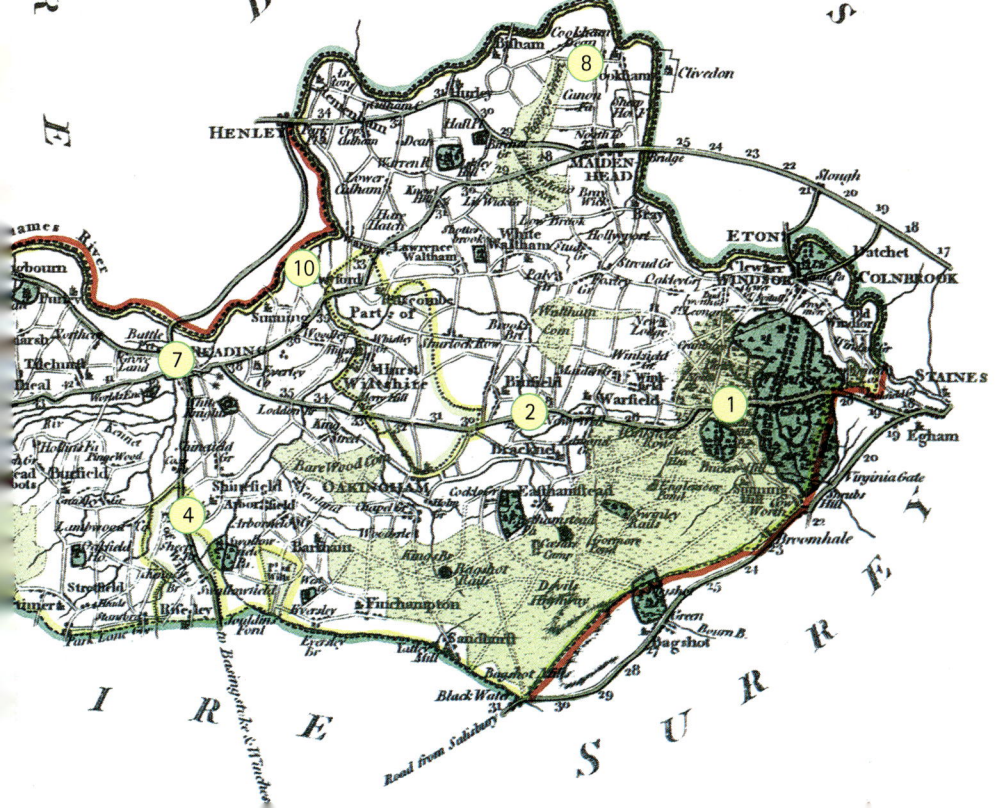

SETTING THE SCENE

Sumer is icumen in,
Lhude sing Cuccu!

THESE EARLY ENGLISH words, set to four-part harmony in c 1250 by a monk in Reading Abbey, celebrate the coming of summer. The writer is thought to have been **John Fornsete** and his delight in the return of warm weather is shared by the creatures of the countryside surrounding the abbey:

Awe bleteth after lomb,
Lhouth after calve cu;
Bulluc sterteth, bucke verteth,
Murie sing cucu!

Both words and music can be seen on a plaque in the abbey ruins, which form part of Walk 7, in central Reading. The route is hardly rural today, but the Abbey Gardens, the River Kennet and the nearby Thames are still home to wildlife, and our spirits lift now, as in 1250, when winter seems to be over.

When John Fornsete and his brother monks lived there, Reading Abbey was at the heart of the county. And of course Berkshire has also, throughout its history, been home to royalty. It has played host, too, to many writers who have come to record royal events or to entertain. It is worth noting here the visits of some of them.

GEOFFREY CHAUCER, 1343/4–1400, probably came to Reading Abbey for the wedding feast of John of Gaunt and Blanche of Lancaster, described in his *The Book of the Duchess*. Chaucer also served as Clerk of Works at Windsor in the reign of Richard II, so it is likely that he lived in the town during that period.

WILLIAM SHAKESPEARE, 1564–1616, knew rural England well and, like the character who sings this verse, probably walked many miles across it:

Jog on, jog on, the footpath way,
And merrily hent the stile-a;
A merry heart goes all the day,
Your sad tires in a mile-a.

In *The Winter's Tale*, Autolycus sings as he walks about the countryside; he, or his creator, reminds us that footpaths and stiles have given folk rights of passage for four hundred years or even for much longer.

Though Shakespeare often includes scenes of country life, in his Berkshire play he shows how people live in towns. In *The Merry Wives of Windsor* exact details are given of the town and the royal parks; whether Shakespeare spent time in Windsor or not, he paints a very clear picture of it.

The Garter Inn, referred to in several scenes in *The Merry Wives of Windsor*, was burnt down in 1681, but Frogmore, featured in Act III, can be visited today, as can Datchet Mead, to which the rascally Falstaff was packed off in a dirty-clothes basket to escape the wrath of Francis Ford. It is not now used for the 'bucking', or bleaching, of linen of course! Plans to curb Falstaff's amorous desires are also made in

Act IV, Scene iv, by the 'merry wives', who use the legend of Herne the Hunter, a former keeper in Windsor Forest who reputedly haunted the Great Oak, where he had committed suicide. Falstaff, disguised like Herne 'with huge horns on his head', was to meet Nan Page near the oak, where most in 'deep night fear to tread'; the children would be dressed 'like urchins, ouphes, and fairies, green and white', with wax tapers and rattles in their hands. They would rush upon Falstaff and torment him with pinches, and the whole party would mock him home to Windsor. Herne's Oak was a famous landmark in the Home Park until 1796, when George III gave orders that all dead trees were to be removed. Later monarchs planted new oaks to keep the legend alive, but their exact locations are difficult to verify.

JOHN BUNYAN, 1628–1688, came to Berkshire as an itinerant preacher, but his Protestantism brought him into danger and he was imprisoned for some months in Reading. His meetings were usually held in a house from which he could escape through a back door and across a bridge over the Kennet. It was during the twelve years he spent in Bedford gaol that Bunyan wrote many religious works, including *The Pilgrim's Progress*. His last visit to Reading came in 1688; he was asked to intercede between a father and son and, when they were reconciled, he preached once more to the Reading congregation. He then rode through heavy rain to a meeting in London, caught a severe chill and died twelve days later.

SAMUEL PEPYS, 1633–1703, came to Windsor on several occasions to carry out official duties. On 19 August 1665 he came to tell the Treasurer of the navy that a disaster had befallen the English fleet at Bergen. In his diary he reports it being a 'very dark night' and he 'got a guide who lost his way in the forest'; in moonlight Pepys himself found the way to Cranbourne and woke the gatekeeper:

> Where in the dark I perceive an old house new building and was fain to go up a ladder to Sir G. Carteret's chamber. And there, in his bed, I sat down, and told him all my bad news, which troubled him mightily; but yet we were very merry, and made the best of it.

Pepys visited Cranbourne Lodge, where Sir Carteret lived, several times; the building needed repair by the 1830s, and much of it was demolished. The single tower that remains is on the route of Walk 1.

Next morning he rose to 'walk forth to see the place; and I find it to be a noble seat in a very noble forest, with the noblest prospect towards Windsor, and round about over many countys, that can be desired'.

In 1666 Pepys was in Windsor Castle to attend a service, where he and his wife sat in the 'knight's stalls'; cushions were brought for them to sit on. On touring the castle he was pleased to see that it was recovering from 'twenty years of neglect and garrisoning' and was impressed by the chapel plate, the knights' robes and the views from the terrace.

DANIEL DEFOE, 1660?–1731, wrote in his *Tour Through England and Wales* that Reading was 'a very large and wealthy

SETTING THE SCENE – WALK 1

town, handsomely-built...the inhabitants rich and driving a very great trade'. There is also an elaborate account of Windsor, so he clearly knew the royal town well, and many of the places he described can still be found.

CHARLES DICKENS, 1812–1870, was well known in Reading; he almost stood for Parliament for the town in 1841 but refused because of the expense. He visited, to give readings from his own work and act in plays, and said it was a faster way to make money than writing novels. He was President of Reading Literary, Scientific and Mechanics Institute, and read to the members in 1854. Life was not all work, however; he declared: 'Rowing down from Oxford to Reading on The Thames is more charming than I can describe in words.'

Although these writers did not live in Berkshire for long, most referred to the county in their plays, poetry or journals and have by their creations made its features known to audiences or readers from their day to this.

Finally, a writer whose link with Berkshire is slightly tenuous:

JOHN MILTON, 1608–1674, lived in Horton in what is now Berkshire but was Buckinghamshire until 1974. Milton left Cambridge at twenty-four and joined his father who had retired to this village near Windsor. In what was then quiet country by the Thames, Milton wrote fine pastoral poetry, *L'Allegro*, *Il Penseroso* and *Lycidas* and his poetic drama, *Comus*. There is a memorial window in Horton Church to the poet and his mother's grave is in the churchyard there.

Walk 1 begins in Windsor Great Park and refers to a number of other writers who walked or rode in it.

WALK 1

A WINDSOR GREAT PARK WALK OF FIVE AND A HALF MILES, TAKING IN SOME PLACES KNOWN TO ALEXANDER POPE, SAMUEL PEPYS AND OTHER WRITERS

Ordnance Survey Landranger Sheet 175
START POINT: grid reference 947727

THE GREAT PARK at Windsor, spreading south and west of the Royal Castle, has given leisure to many visitors, both royal and the less exalted, throughout history. Not surprisingly, many writers have walked or ridden along its leafy ways, noted its grandeur or used it in their work. In one of his plays Ben Jonson names two of his characters Prue of the Park and Frances of the Castle, while Jonathan Swift reported that Queen Anne 'was hunting the stag till four this afternoon, and she drove in her chaise forty miles, and it was five before we went to dinner'. Shakespeare wrote about the town of Windsor, its parks and Datchet Stream, as mentioned earlier. The forest events in *The Merry Wives of Windsor* were set in what is now called The Home Park. Since Queen Victoria's day, this park has been open to the public only on special occasions. However, to walk or ride in The Great Park, except in motor vehicles, has been allowed from earliest times.

Walk 1 visits areas in Windsor Great Park where Alexander Pope often rode, with Sir William Trumbull, through scenery that inspired his important poem 'Windsor

SETTING THE SCENE – WALK 1

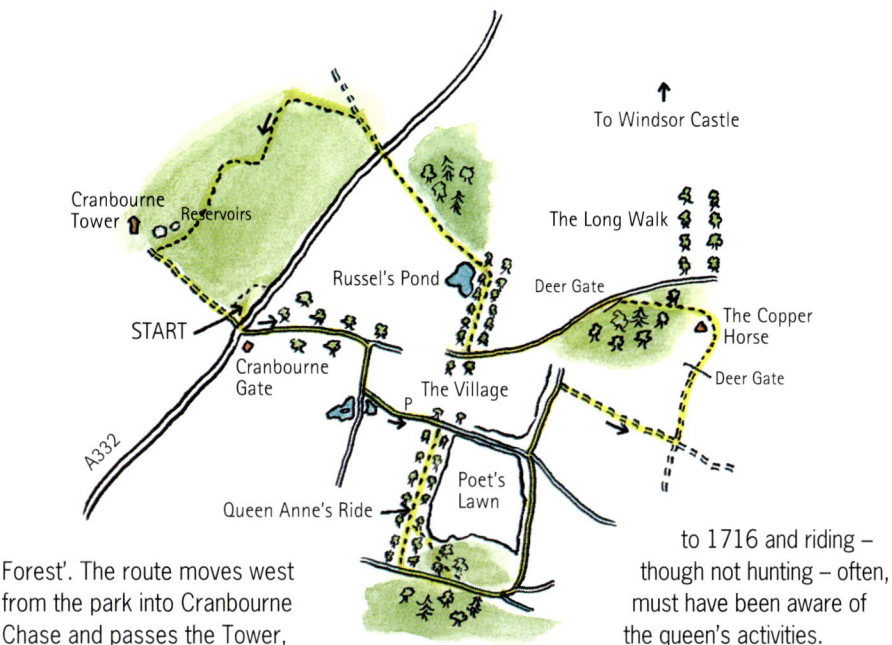

WINDSOR GREAT PARK

Forest'. The route moves west from the park into Cranbourne Chase and passes the Tower, all that remains of Cranbourne Lodge, which was visited by Pepys in 1665.

Begin from the car parking area opposite Cranbourne Gate, in Sheet Street Road (A332), about a mile from the south end of Sheet Street Road at [GR 947727] above Forest Lodge. Cross the road and enter the park at Cranbourne Gate. Walk ahead on the grass verge. Some of the fine trees in the vicinity commemorate events such as Queen Victoria's Golden Jubilee in 1887 and Edward VII's coronation in 1902.

Turn right at the crossroads, then left before two ponds, and walk towards The Village. Pass the Post Office, or perhaps pause to take refreshment, then walk to where Queen Anne's Ride, marked by young trees, crosses the road. Turn right into this Ride, created by Queen Anne in 1703 so that she could drive her chaise to hunting grounds near Ascot. Pope, living in Binfield from 1701 to 1716 and riding – though not hunting – often, must have been aware of the queen's activities.

As you walk, climbing gently, you have on the left Poet's Lawn, where Pope reputedly rode among the trees. In his day it was turfed, but now you may well see crops growing here. Walk to the top and turn left on to a tarmac drive. Turn left at the next junction and walk ahead on the grass verge, with Poet's Lawn again on your left, to where roads cross; here go ahead, with Richard's Lawn on your left. Take the first turning on the right, which is a wide, hedged, grassy path, then turn left up a broad, hedged, grass ride.

Walk through a deer gate and continue up to the Copper Horse statue. Astride the horse, enjoying even finer views than we do, is a bronze George III, put there in 1831 by George IV, his son. You may have caught glimpses of Windsor Castle earlier; now you will see it clearly ahead, at the far end of the Long Walk. This three-mile, oak-

11

SETTING THE SCENE – WALK 1

Cranbourne Tower.

lined avenue was established in the 1680s. Daniel Defoe called it 'a noble walk', and Dean Swift described it as 'the finest avenue I ever saw'.

To continue the walk, turn left as you face the castle, to enter a path under trees. This widens to a track and drops down to reach a deer gate at the road. Through the gate, walk left and take a wider road ahead that bends slightly right. Follow this road until, just before a house on the left, Queen Anne's Ride crosses it; you will notice that young trees have been planted to replace some of the original ones. Turn right into

the Ride. Pass Russel's Pond on the left, then take a fenced path on the left. Fork left up a wide path, passing woodland on the right, then continue down to reach Ranger's Gate and the A332; cross this main road again with care.

Take the tarmac drive opposite. Beyond two large trees, veer left on a bridleway, through the trees. At the top of the slope, where the sandy track bends left, leave it to follow a grass path until you almost reach a gate; here turn left, continue by a right-hand fence to reach Cranbourne Tower on the right. This fine structure, built about five hundred years ago, was part of the imposing lodge visited by Pepys in 1665 and another diarist, John Evelyn, in 1673. Pope, too, would have seen the lodge while out riding, but in the 1800s unsafe parts of the building were removed, leaving only the tower, where Queen Victoria and other royal visitors would pause for tea.

Turn away from the tower and take the drive back to the car parking area. On the way, notice how splendid the ancient oaks are. In the 1500s Queen Elizabeth I had thirteen acres of Cranbourne Walk sown with acorns, which 'forty years later became a wood of some thousands of tall, young oaks'. Could some of these still be standing today?

ALEXANDER POPE, 1688–1744

I often give a Range to my Imagination, and goe a strolling with one or other of you, up and down Binfield Wood, or over Bagshot Heath.

SO WROTE THE renowned writer, Alexander Pope, in February 1717, after he had moved away from his friends in Berkshire. Pope lived in Berkshire during his most formative years, and some of his finest poetry was inspired by the Windsor Forest, which he loved. Names such as Popeswood, Popeswood Road and Pope's Manor on maps of this part of the county are reminders of the years 1701 to 1716 when the writer's home was in Binfield, which at that time was part of the forest.

The Pope family chose to retire to the Windsor Forest area, and later to leave it, because of the political turbulence of the time. The poet's father, a Roman Catholic merchant in the City of London, saw much to alarm him in the anti-papist feelings, plots and executions of the time. Catholics were also given few rights, and were wise to live quietly and to choose their friendships carefully.

Alexander was born in May 1688, in the same year that Protestant William III came from Holland to take over the English throne. Edith, Alexander's mother, was his father's second wife, his first wife having died in childbirth. His father's firstborn son, also called Alexander, died at an early age while in the care of Pope's Aunt Mary, who lived in Pangbourne. The new son was therefore especially dear to his parents. He grew up, a child among fond adults, in a substantial house in Plough Court, Lombard Street, in the City of London; he was taught to read by an aunt, and by the age of seven had learned Latin and some Greek from a priest living with the family. Catholics could not practise their religion and their children were not allowed to attend public schools or universities. In private, however, worship continued and there were some small schools with Catholic teachers. Samuel Johnson, in his *Lives of the English Poets*, acidly wrote of one such school that Pope attended: 'How Mr Deane could spend, with a boy who had translated so much of Ovid, some months over a small part of Tully's Offices, it is now vain to enquire.' He goes on to describe how Pope, at the age of twelve, decided to direct his own study, 'which he completed with little other incitement than the desire of excellence'.

ALEXANDER POPE

It was to Berkshire, then, that the young Pope came to carry out his own education. Royal Windsor Forest was vast, far larger than today; it comprised woods with rides, farms with meadows, and wide stretches of heathland. Within this forest, the Pope family settled in Binfield, in what was then called Whitehill House. This house was modest in comparison with Easthampstead, Whiteknights and many other residences occupied by the county's leading families. Pope in a later poem called *Whitehill*:

> *A little House with trees a-row,*
> *And like its Master, very low.*

He described his years in Binfield as 'the happiest time of my life'. His *Pastoral Poem II, Summer*, although it owes a little to his study of Virgil, glows with delight in the countryside he found around him:

> *O deign to visit our forsaken seats,*
> *The mossy fountains and the cool retreats!*
>
> *Where'er you walk, cool gales shall fan the glade;*
> *Trees, where you sit, shall crowd into a shade;*
> *Where'er you tread, the blushing flow'rs shall rise,*
> *And all things flourish where you turn your eyes.*

The 'Little House with Trees a-row' from a print of 1852. Part of this house remains within the present house known as 'Pope's Manor'.

To introduce his own poems to the reader, in 1704, at sixteen years of age, Pope wrote a learned preface on the pastoral form as used by Greek and Roman poets and in the sixteenth century by Edmund Spenser. 'What is inviting in this sort of poetry proceeds', he claims, 'from the tranquility of a country life.' There should be description of 'the most agreeable objects of the country', written in language 'the smoothest, the most easy and flowing imaginable'.

The twenty-acre estate of woods and meadows that surrounded Whitehill House gave the young Pope plenty of opportunity to study the scenery and wildlife. It also provided quiet places for reading. To the north of the house, in the area of the present Popeswood Road, a slope crowned with a copse of mature beech trees was a favoured retreat; in fine weather, according to local legend, Pope took his books and writing materials here. In later years, visitors came to see the tree inscribed 'Here Pope sung'.

To widen the range of his own diligent study, the young poet drew on the knowledge of classics of his literary friends. It was fortunate that Sir William Trumbull lived a few miles from Binfield, at Easthamstead Park. Sir William shared the elder Pope's love of gardening and admired that gentleman's ability to grow artichokes of great size; to the son, half a century his junior, he became an affectionate mentor and companion. His distinguished Oxford University years had been followed by a career in diplomacy and travel to cultural centres in France and Italy; he sent to London for copies of books, such as *Milton's Minor Poems* (1645), and helped his 'precocious little neighbour' in his literary plans.

From the age of thirteen Pope began to suffer from bone tuberculosis and increasingly this threatened to cripple him; medical advice prescribed that he should 'apply less and ride every day'. Sir William, a verderer of the forest, had to make regular inspections, so he was an ideal riding partner for the poet, whose health did improve for a time. Lines from *Windsor Forest* illustrate this:

Happy the man, who to these shades retires,
Whom nature charms, and who the muse inspires:
He gathers health from herbs the forest yields,
And of their fragrant physic spoil the fields.

In about 1704, Pope began work on this poem, which was to be one of his finest; during rides with Trumbull the scenery and themes were planned. The poem was to extol the seasonal pleasures and rich resources of rural England, and to celebrate the history and heroes of Windsor Forest in particular. As ideas developed, the Thames was shown to draw the riches of the Shires and carry them in trade to Europe and beyond. That prosperity resulted, when Tory agricultural achievements were combined with Whig mercantile skills, gave the poem the theme of peace. Sir William Trumbull's local knowledge helped the poet; he gave details of Berkshire rivers:

The winding Isis and the fruitful Thame;
The Kennet swift, for silver eels renowned;
The Loddon slow, with verdant alders crowned;

As a keen fisherman, who had 'eyed the dancing cork and bending reed' for many years, Trumbull could well have shared the secrets of his craft:

The bright-ey'd perch with fins of Tyrian dye,
The silver eel, in shining volumes roll'd,
The yellow carp, in scales bedropp'd with gold,
Swift trouts, diversified with crimson stains,
And pikes, the tyrants of the watery plains.

Pope does not suggest that fishing is cruel but he has no time for those who shoot birds in the name of sport:

See! from the break the whirring pheasant springs,
And mounts exulting on triumphant wings:
Short is his joy; he feels the fiery wound,
Flutters in blood, and panting beats the ground.

Perhaps the poet had seen, too closely, 'clamorous lapwings' feel 'leaden death' or the 'mounting larks' as they fell 'leave their little lives in air.' It is quite often poets who have changed attitudes to such cruelty.

Pope knew and worked with most of the leading literary figures of the age. John Dryden (1631–1700) was revered, as were earlier poets, Shakespeare and Milton; he kept their pictures in his rooms, that the 'constant remembrance' of them 'may keep me always humble'. William Wycherley was in his sixties when Pope met him in 1704; although his plays were often staged, he could not get his poetry published and the young poet, whose *Pastorals* had received such favourable notice, decided to help. Wycherley visited Binfield at least once; the heavily built, elderly dramatist and the delicate, stooping young poet made a strange couple, as they walked along deep in discussion.

The eminent and versatile writer Jonathan Swift also valued the young man's work: in a letter in 1713 he says: 'Mr Pope has published a fine poem called *Windsor Forest*; read it.' Swift was a co-founder with Pope of Scriblerus Club, which aimed to satirise the artistic and political follies of the age. When Queen Anne died in 1714, Tories like Swift lost favour; he retreated to a friend's parsonage at Letcombe Bassett, where Pope visited him with poet Thomas Parnell. It rained hard; Pope's neat parody in pastoral form states:

Yet Dew or Rain may wett us to the shift
We'll not be slow to visit Dr Swift...

Dean Swift returned to Ireland and in the next ten years expanded the themes of Scriblerus into *Gulliver's Travels*. Pope had regular witty correspondence with him for twenty-six years. In 1714 he wrote: 'If I writ this in verse, I would tell you, you are like the sun, and, while men imagine you to be retir'd or absent, are hourly exerting your influence, and bringing things to maturity for their advantage.'

Pope entertained many literary friends at Binfield. Henry Cromwell, a poet who was something of a dandy, visited in 1711; Pope said in a letter that his visit had been so popular with the ladies they 'look on us as plain Country fellows since they saw you, and heard more civil things in one Fortnight than they expect from the whole Shire of us, in an age.' Nicholas Rowe, whose edition of Shakespeare's plays Pope admired, stayed for a week in 1713. John Gay, whose greatest triumph was to be his *Beggar's Opera* of 1728, was a frequent guest; Pope gave him support throughout

ALEXANDER POPE

his life. He writes in 1714: 'you have a warm corner in my heart, and a retreat at Binfield in the worst of times is at your service.' Some occasions were jolly also; Pope, Swift and Gay spent one wet summer day in the Rose Inn, Wokingham, composing verses to 'sweet Molly Mog', the landlord's daughter.

The Pope family made many friends in the local Catholic community. The manor of Binfield was the Dancastle family home and the Whiteknights estate belonged to the Englefields. These families gave much support to the young poet; Thomas Dancastle made fair copies of Pope's draft texts and Anthony Englefield, learned and lively, introduced him to some most valued friends. The Shakespearian actor Thomas Betterton had retired to a farm on the Whiteknights estate: Pope's love of drama grew and, when the actor died in 1710, he became his literary executor and prepared his Chaucerian adaptations for publication for the benefit of his widow. Some Englefield relatives became firm friends. Pope's letters to John Caryll seem to reveal his inner feelings; they shared literary activities and it was John Caryll who suggested that Pope should write a poem to heal the rift that resulted when Robert Lord Petre cut off a lock of Arabella Fermor's hair. Society's foibles were parodied delightfully in *The Rape of the Lock*; the poem, published in its full version in 1714 when Pope was still only twenty-six, is a comic masterpiece. It delights readers still, so its last lines are prophetic:

> *When those fair suns shall set, as set they must,*
> *And all those tresses shall be laid in dust,*
> *This Lock the Muse shall consecrate to fame,*
> *And 'midst the stars inscribe Belinda's name.*

...and Pope's, too, of course!

Some of Pope's best-known friends lived in countryside near the Thames; Antony Englefield's granddaughters, Teresa and Martha Blount, lived at Mapledurham, on the river west of Reading. Teresa, dark-haired and vivacious, was two years older than the shy, fair, book-loving Martha. According to family tradition, Pope first met the two sisters in 1707; he visited them often and sent jolly letters to them when they moved to London in 1715. That autumn he wrote:

> Dear Ladies, You have here all the Fruit Mr. Dancastle's garden affords that I could find in any degree of ripeness. They were on the Trees at eleven this morning, and I hope will be with you before night. Pray return, sealed up, by the bearer, every single bit of paper that wraps 'em up: for they are the Only Copies of this part of Homer. If the fruit is not as good as I wish, let the Gallantry of this Wrapping-paper make up for it. I'm Yours

Neither sister married, nor did Pope; Martha was a close friend all his life and

ALEXANDER POPE – WALK 2

he left her much of his property. A month before his death he wrote, 'I have little to say to you when we meet, but I love you upon unalterable principles, which makes me feel my heart the same to you as if I saw you every hour. Adieu.' Portraits of Martha, Teresa and Pope can be seen in Mapledurham House, together with some of Pope's books and furniture.

The pages of Homer referred to in the 1715 letter to the Blount sisters were part of the most ambitious work undertaken by Pope during his years in Berkshire. In 1713 he announced his intention to translate and publish the entire *Iliad* in a subscription edition in six volumes at a guinea each, 'printed...on the finest paper, with Ornaments and initial Letters engraven on Copper'. He was well supported in this plan; the first volume appeared in June 1715 and the second in March 1716. Later volumes were completed in Chiswick or in Twickenham, because when Hanoverian George I came to the throne on Queen Anne's death in 1714, life became yet more restricted for those considered to be Papist. By April 1716 Pope's family had sold the house at Binfield and moved to Chiswick under the protection of a prominent Whig, Richard Boyle. To Parnell, who had returned to Ireland, Pope wrote: 'Binfield, alas! is no more and the Muse is driven from those forests of which she sang.'

In 1719, after his father's death, he bought a home for himself and his mother at Twickenham; here, until his death in 1744, his Muse continued to lead him to more and more literary achievements.

Because of his ill-health, Pope could not walk the distances covered by some writers who have lived in Berkshire, but he was active. Life in the country meant 'morning walks' by 'purling brooks' and reference in letters shows how usual it was for him to ramble about Binfield with his spaniel, 'a little one, a lean one, and none of the finest Shap'd', he tells Henry Cromwell, hinting that the dog was like its master. In 1713 he tells Caryll, 'I have just been taking a solitary walk by moonshine', and he teases the Blount sisters in 1717, 'Mrs Lepell walk'd all alone with me three or four hours, by moonlight'.

Named 'the little Nightingale' or 'the Swan of Windsor' by fellow poets, Pope undoubtedly loved strolling or riding in the forest or by the Thames; he called his years in Berkshire 'The happiest part of my life'. He told Martha Blount in 1734 that he planned to 'look on Whiteknights' and 'lay in Windsor Forest at Mr Dancastle's' as 'This may be the last time I shall see those Scenes of my past Life, where I have been so happy'.

WALK 2

A SHORT WALK OF ABOUT A MILE, CIRCLING THE BINFIELD HOME OF ALEXANDER POPE

Ordnance Survey Landranger Sheet 175
START POINT: grid reference 845696

ALTHOUGH THE NAME Pope appears in so many forms on the map of Berkshire, the routes through the Forest that the poet walked and rode along have suffered changes. The 'little house with Trees a-row', although altered, does remain, however, and a small part of the twenty acres farmed

ALEXANDER POPE – WALK 2

by the family is preserved as a public open space, as this short ramble shows.

The walk begins from London Road, the A329, at its junction with St Mark's Road at Binfield. There is a bus-stop (marked BS on the map [below]) near this junction, and, if you need to travel by car, there is a car park at Pope's Meadow, off St Mark's Road, about two hundred yards from the traffic lights (marked P on the map). If you are starting from the car park, complete the walk by entering the gate near the traffic lights at the end of the circuit.

Walk into St Mark's Road at the traffic lights, then immediately through a gate on the left, at Ramblers' Route signs. Already you are walking in part of the garden of Whitehill House, as Pope's Manor was called in his day. Follow the path between holly and laurels under tall trees; to the left the Manor and ponds can be seen. At a fingerpost, where the fence ends, turn left to pass a pond and enter Pope's Meadow. Managed by Bracknell Forest Borough Council, this grassy place, with its tall trees and seats, is a valued quiet space.

Walk along the right-hand side of the field, passing a picnic area, then make for a gate to the left in the north-west corner. This leads to Murrellhill Lane, where you turn left. In spite of nearby busy roads, this lane runs along quietly between Pope's Meadow and fields sometimes grazed by sheep.

Walk ahead to reach Pope's Manor, which is now owned by the Bryant Group; the house that Pope lived in between 1701 and 1716 forms the core of the imposing building that is visible today. The grounds are open to visitors occasionally. Further along the lane, on the right-hand side, are buildings called Pope's Farm. Continue to the junction and turn left into London Road to return to the start.

This is a walk of about a mile; a section of a much longer Ramblers' Route that circles Bracknell passes Easthampstead Park, where Pope's mentor Sir William Trumbull lived; details of this walk and of any open days at Pope's Manor are available from Bracknell Forest Borough Council Leisure Services.

Walk 1, in Windsor Park, also has reference to Pope.

19

JANE AUSTEN, 1775–1817

JANE AUSTEN LIVED for only a short time in Berkshire but she deserves to be included in this book as she attended boarding school in Reading, she often stayed with close friends and relatives in this county, she enjoyed walking and she also wrote much in praise of the countryside of southern England.

Of Jane Austen's published letters, most were written to her sister, Cassandra; between discussion of domestic details and parties there are reports of forays on foot. In May 1801, for instance, she wrote to Cassandra in Kintbury from Bath:

> Our grand walk to Weston was again fixed for Yesterday...it would have amused you to see our progress; we went up by Sion Hill & returned across the fields; in climbing a hill Mrs Chamberlyne is very capital; I could with difficulty keep pace with her – yet would not flinch for the world. – On plain ground I was quite her equal...

A week later Cassandra is given details of her sister's next outing with the Bath lady, well-known for her walking prowess:

> I walked yesterday morning with Mrs Chamberlyne to Lyncombe & Widcombe...her pace was not quite so magnificent on this second trial, as on the first; it was nothing more than I could keep up with, without effort; and for many, many yards together on a raised narrow footpath I led the way. The walk was very beautiful, as my companion agreed, whenever I made the observation...

The gentle humour does not hide Jane's enjoyment of her exercise. She was born in the country, into a large and loving family. With parents of learning and culture, she, her sister and six brothers grew up amidst an even wider circle of supportive relatives and friends.

Jane first lived away from home when she was seven; she, her sister and her cousin Jane Cooper were sent to school in Oxford. An outbreak of fever after the school moved to Southampton resulted in their return home. Two years later, in 1785, when Jane was nearly ten, the three girls again left their homes for school, this time in Reading. The school for young ladies, run by Mrs La Tournelle, was housed in the inner gatehouse of Reading's ruined abbey; this lady also rented a large adjoining house and garden. The gatehouse had a room above its arch, reached by staircases with balustrades that had originally been gilded. From the embankment that ran around part of the garden, the girls could look down on ruins of what had once been 'third in size and wealth of all English abbeys'. Mrs La Tournelle conducted her pupils through the varied, but hardly academic, activities usual for the high fees charged. Judging by a later sale of its assets, the school was well-equipped however, with many books, globes and even an early epidiascope. As explained in Walk 7, in central Reading, the abbey gatehouse was rebuilt by Gilbert Scott in 1861 and, as pictures of the original archway show, some original features were retained. The room above the arch, where lessons were taught, is today a meeting room, and some of the original Norman stone stairways appear to have survived within the Victorian reconstruction.

The pupils seem to have enjoyed plenty of freedom. They had formal lessons in the mornings and in the afternoons had time to enjoy the sunny garden or follow their own interests. Jane had learned to read at an early age, so is likely to have found the lending library, which existed then in the nearby marketplace, a source of much pleasure. A dancing master taught ballroom skills and the older girls were joined by boys from Dr Valpy's Reading School for evening parties. When Edward Austen and Edward Cooper visited their sisters they were even allowed to take them out for dinner at a local inn. Pleasant as it seems to have

Reading Abbey gateway.

been, schooling in Reading lasted for only two years; by 1787 Jane and Cassandra were back home in Steventon. There Jane thrived; to augment his income, Mr Austen acted as tutor to young men hoping to enter university, so his daughters imbibed an atmosphere that encouraged study and the use of his extensive library.

Anna, a niece of Jane and Cassandra, remembers that they had a bedroom and sitting room on the first floor with 'Jane's piano' and Cassandra's painting materials; on the bookshelves were Samuel Richardson's novel *Clarissa* and various poetry collections. As well as classical authors, Jane Austen read contemporary writers such as Henry Fielding, Oliver Goldsmith, Laurence Sterne and Dr Johnson. Most members of her talented family were involved with writing of some kind, so none were surprised that Jane was too. By twelve, she had written the prologues for family theatrical performances and had filled three quarto notebooks with witty fiction.

Jane Austen also came to Berkshire for reasons other than schooling; it is likely she visited her mother's brother, James Leigh Perrot, and his wife, who lived in a fine house called Scarlets, at Hare Hatch, not far from Maidenhead on the Reading Road. Her mother's sister, Jane, and husband, Reverend Edward Cooper, also lived at Sonning from 1784. Most often, however, she stayed at the rectory in Kintbury, west of Newbury, on the Kennet and Avon Canal. This was where the Fowle family lived; the two eldest sons were Mr Austen's pupils and friends of the Austen children. Cassandra was engaged to Tom Fowle, so Jane often wrote to her at Kintbury and also stayed there. Tom died of yellow fever in the West Indies, where he had hoped, as chaplain to Lord Craven's troops, to earn sufficient income to marry. James Austen wrote to recall happy times spent at Kintbury:

Where sloping uplands catch the sun's first beam,
Where winding through the meadow,
Kennet's stream
Reflects an outline true, but tint less bright,
The grey Church tower, tall tree and Mansion white.

He ends with sorrow, as he muses by 'the green and willowed shore' and thinks on 'joys that can return no more'. The white rectory, where for the young people of both families there was enjoyment as well as sorrow, was replaced by a new, larger one in the 1860s. The church, the Kennet and some houses, however, remain little changed. Jane Austen enjoyed passing on, with her usual wit, news about those who lived in this part of Berkshire. In a letter of 1801 to Cassandra, she says that Eliza Fowle

> has seen Lord Craven at Barton, & probably by this time at Kintbury, where he was expected for one day this week. She found his manners very pleasing indeed. The little flaw of having a Mistress now living with him at Ashdown Park, seems to be the only unpleasing circumstance about him.

Barton Court, home then of the Dundas family, is half a mile beyond the Kennet to the north, and Ashdown House is about fourteen miles further to the north-west.

JANE AUSTEN

Many journeys took Jane Austen through Berkshire; in May 1813 she writes she is to go to Windsor, en route to Henley, 'which will be delightful'. Reading was often a staging post and later in 1813 she writes that they 'will get no further on Thursday and so, reach Steventon by a reasonable dinner hour the next day'. Visits for pleasure were also made to this county; letters mention the assembly and races at Newbury, for example. Places very close to Berkshire also gave her inspiration. Monthly dances were held in the Assembly Room above the stables of the Angel Inn in Basingstoke; here a mixture of people from the market town and surrounding villages provided an observant young novelist with characters to people her stories and a range of situations and dilemmas to pose. Her acquaintance with some very fine houses and estates was gained in Kent, where Godmersham was inherited by her brother Edward, but also in houses nearer home – The Vyne in Hampshire, for example, just south of the Berkshire border. Jane's brother James became vicar of a parish neighbouring The Vyne estate and when he became friendly with the Chute family she was included in visits to them. In a diary entry for April 1799, Mrs Chute records 'Jane Austen dined'; although wealthy, the family lived quietly, giving only two or three dinner parties yearly, so to attend was a privilege. She also often visited Ibthorpe House, south-west of Newbury, the home of close friends Mary and Martha Lloyd; here the chalk downs and deeply wooded vales suited such 'desperate walkers' as Jane and Martha.

Set in a world that was familiar to her, and reflecting moral values and views that were formed by it, the novels of Jane Austen picture an ideal period in the history of the English countryside, its villages and market towns. Mrs Goddard's 'real, honest old-fashioned boarding school', in *Emma*, was approved of and is likely to have been based on Jane's time in Reading:

Mrs Goddard's school was held in high repute and very deservedly; for Highbury was reckoned a very healthy spot; she had an ample house and garden, gave the children plenty of wholesome food ...

and

... let them run about a great deal in the summer ...in fact a reasonable quantity of accomplishments were sold at a reasonable price.

Ideal villages exist in most of Jane Austen's novels; Uppercross in *Persuasion* 'is a moderate-sized village, the mansion of the squire, with its high walls, great gates and old trees, substantial and unmodernised, and the compact tight parsonage, enclosed in its own neat garden, with a vine and pear-tree trained round its casements'.

Well-managed estates, such as Mr Knightley's Donwell, in *Emma*, cared for by sound tenant-farmers like Robert Martin, are the backbone of Jane Austen's perfect landscapes, and she would have walked from village to village, storing images of wooded hills and churches nestling in the valleys. If we, as today's ramblers, will admit it, our idea of perfect countryside is much the same as in her day.

Characters in Jane Austen's novels who are portrayed as having sound moral values not surprisingly share her own views, and often have greater means than she had of acting on them. She mocks clergy who trade in livings, seeing them as a means to take part in the society of the 'big house', and keeps her approval for Edmund Bertram in *Mansfield Park*, whose faith, work and quiet wife, Fanny, will give parishioners the support that is their due. Elizabeth, in *Pride and Prejudice*, puts concern for her ill sister before regard for what society expects; she walks through fields to Netherfield to the amazement of the two Miss Bingleys, as the elder exclaims:

> 'To walk three miles, or four miles, or five miles, or whatever it is, above her ankles in dirt, and alone, quite alone! It seems to me to show an abominable sort of conceited independence, a most country town indifference to decorum.'
> 'It shews an affection for her sister that is very pleasing,' said Bingley.
> 'I am afraid, Mr Darcy,' observed Miss Bingley, 'that this adventure has rather affected your admiration of her fine eyes.'
> 'Not at all,' he replied; 'they were brightened by the exercise.'

By the conclusion of the novel, it is neither of the Bingley sisters but Elizabeth who has won the eligible Mr Darcy!

Most of Jane Austen's characters walk for both exercise and enjoyment; the Dashwood sisters, on their rambles in *Sense and Sensibility*, explore the country lanes or climb the downs and valleys almost every day for: 'The whole country around them abounded in beautiful walks.' In *Persuasion* the Musgrove sisters planned 'a long walk' with romance in view. Six young men and women set out; of these Anne Elliot felt her 'pleasure in the walk must arise from the exercise and the day, from the view of the last smiles of the year upon the tawny leaves and withered hedges'.

However, it is by means of informal events such as this, and a walk along the Cobb at Lyme later in the same novel, that Jane Austen advances the plot and Anne finds that she has not, after all, missed her chance for happiness.

Jane Austen, her mother and sister settled in Chawton, near Alton in Hampshire, in 1809: all her major novels were written or revised for publication there. Although none of the books published in her lifetime named the author, she became well known and admired. The Prince Regent kept a set of her works in each one of his houses, and *Emma* was 'respectfully dedicated' to him. Henry Austen arranged the publication of *Northanger Abbey* and *Persuasion* after his sister's death in July 1817. Sir Walter Scott, in 1837, wrote in his journal that he had just read *Pride and Prejudice* for the third time; he said that he could write in 'The Big Bow-wow strain...but the exquisite touch, which renders ordinary commonplace things and characters interesting, from the truth of the description and the sentiment, is denied me.'

Jane Austen is buried in Winchester Cathedral. Before her final illness, she enjoyed a busy period, writing, playing her piano, visiting, and being visited by, relatives and friends. She did some of the gardening at Chawton Cottage, and the nearby countryside, where she walked almost every day of her life, continued to delight her.

JANE AUSTEN – WALK 3

WALK 3

A JANE AUSTEN WALK OF SIX MILES, STARTING FROM KINTBURY, WHICH REFERS ALSO TO RICHARD ADAMS AND ROBERT HARRIS

Ordnance Survey Landranger Sheet 174
START POINT: grid reference 385672

IN THE SOUTH-WEST corner of Berkshire, Kintbury and its surrounding countryside offers pleasant walking. Jane Austen knew this well, for she and her sister, Cassandra, often stayed in the rectory at Kintbury with the Reverend Thomas Fowle, his wife, Jane, and their four clever sons. Walking was a favoured pastime.

This walk of about six miles, taking in waterside, hills and views, is likely to have been one of those taken by the young Austens and their friends; James Austen's lines, quoted above, describe days spent 'rambling and swimming together' in Berkshire.

Kintbury lies a mile south of the A4, about halfway between Newbury and Hungerford. Begin the walk from a canalside public car park just south of the level crossing, on the opposite side of the road from the station. On weekdays Kintbury can be reached by train.

Walk to the canal and the lock. This length of waterway was completed in 1797, so Jane Austen could have seen it being built. From the lock, cross Station Road and walk east along the towpath. The River Kennet flows in several channels here and one runs on the left, edged by a path that is now private, as is the woodland beyond it.

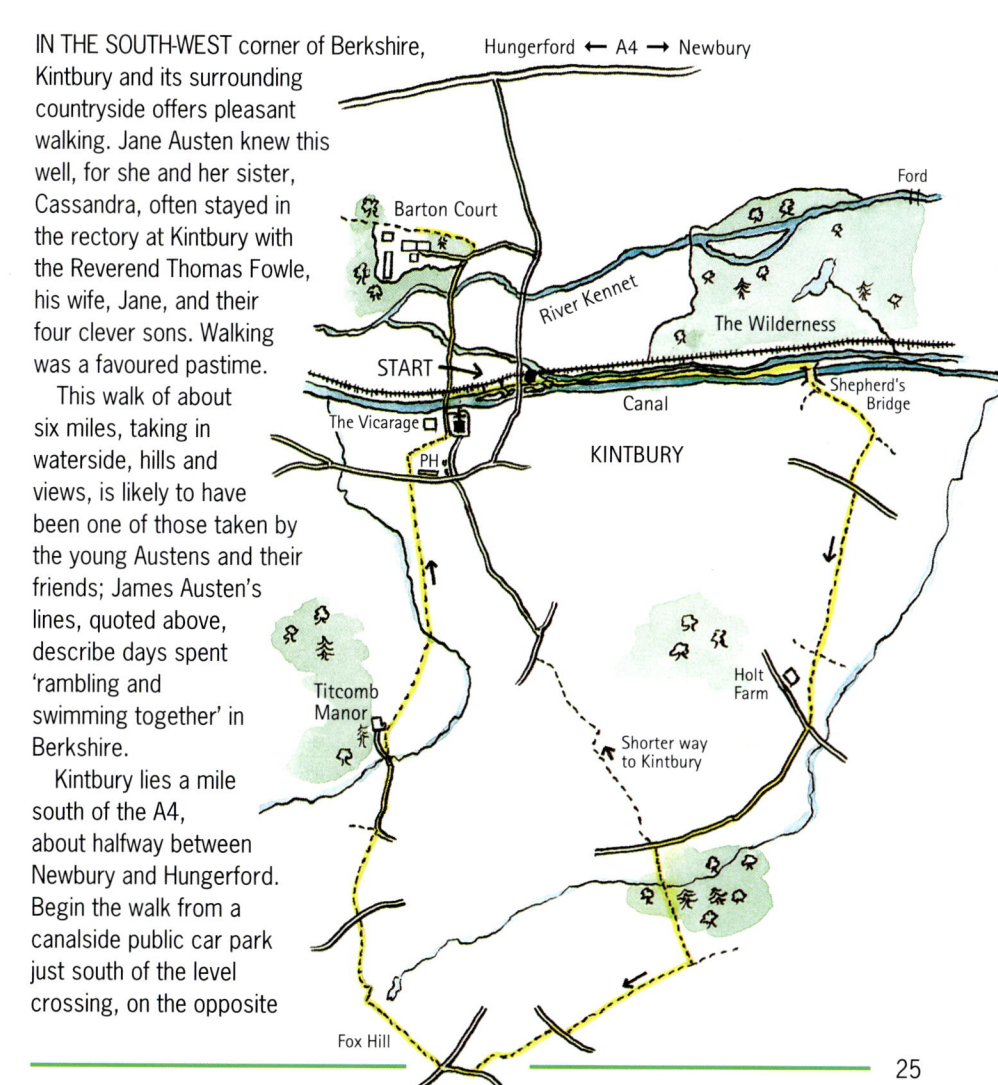

25

This, called The Wilderness, is where Richard Adams, author of *Watership Down*, as a boy, saw his first kingfisher (see page 103). Walk along the towpath for three-quarters of a mile, then cross the canal by the bridge. Take a footpath ahead up a hill; at the top a backward look gives a fine view of The Wilderness and, perhaps, narrow boats passing along the canal.

At footpath signs, follow the right-hand one downhill, cross the lane at the bottom and enter the footpath ahead. Ignore a crossing path and at Holt Farm go ahead to reach a road. Take a lane opposite signposted Inkpen and walk ahead, ignoring the first path sign on the left, but taking the next left (for a shortcut back to Kintbury, take the path opposite, to the right). To continue the main walk, cross the stile on the left, walk down through the meadow, cross a brook, turn left over the next stile and follow a winding path through a copse to emerge at a field; turn right along the headland and left at the field corner. At the path junction go right to a stile, then walk ahead across a meadow, along a fenced patch and through a field with stiles between each, to reach a road. Here walk a few steps to the right and, opposite, cross a footbridge and stile into another field. A short way before the end of this field cross double stiles on the right, walk diagonally left, cross another double stile, then walk ahead to pass a small cottage and enter a lane.

Turn right at the lane, and cross a road ahead to a broad gravel drive. When this drive bears left, enter a footpath ahead; it leads between gardens to a path beyond a five-barred gate in the far corner. Follow this path, which curves left to a metal gate giving access to a road. Across the road take the signed path between properties and cross a stile into a field. There are good views of the Kennet Valley. Walk down two fields with a squeeze stile and a gate, to reach a small lane at Titcomb. Do not follow a left-pointing footpath sign but walk down the lane and, as it turns left, see beyond a drive Titcomb Manor. This is one of five Kintbury Manors recorded in the Domesday survey; at that time, in lieu of rent, tenants had to keep a hawk ready for the king's hunting. Peacocks can be heard now, as the walker passes.

To return to Kintbury, turn right into a field, then go along by the hedge on your left to footpath signs; follow the one that points right and, with trees on your left, reach a stile and cross it into another field. Now keeping to the hedge on the right, walk ahead to cross a stile in the right-hand corner of the field. Follow the fenced path to reach and cross a footbridge and stile, at the field end. Take a few steps right, go over another stile, then take the fenced path to reach High Street, Kintbury. Across the road on the right is the Blue Ball, which may be a welcome stopping place. Alternatively, take a path to the left of the inn, then go right between houses to reach Church Road, where, a few steps to the right, are Dippins Tea Rooms.

To complete the walk, continue left to St Mary's Church, where there are memorials to some of Jane Austen's friends; she came to services in St Mary's and named in the list of the vicars since 1303 are three of the Fowles family. A guide book gives more details of people she would have known. From the church take the path that drops towards the canal; on the left stood the vicarage where Jane Austen stayed. Only a painting remains of the original building. Kintbury continues to have literary links; best-selling author Robert Harris now lives in the village.

Over the canal bridge and down steps to the right, you can return to the towpath and the car park, but to follow further in Jane Austen's footsteps, on walks she almost certainly would have taken, do not take the steps down just yet but keep ahead along the wide footpath, crossing more flows of the Kennet. After about half a mile there is a good view of Barton Court.

Complete the walk by retracing your steps to the car park at Kintbury.

MARY RUSSELL MITFORD, 1787–1855

AMONG ALL THE writers who have lived in Berkshire, Mary Russell Mitford holds a special place. With insight and humour she depicted the county's quiet villages and bustling towns – with their people of all walks of life – at a time when it was more customary to write mainly about the nobility. She lived in Reading, Grazeley, Three Mile Cross and Swallowfield for almost all her life. She is now best known as the author of *Our Village*, in which she describes the activities in the street below her window; she depicts her garden and the nearby lanes, where she loved to walk; and she shares her delight in the friendships made there. In the first chapter she takes us on a walk in Three Mile Cross, with its cottages, farms and inn; we meet the villagers and the settings of their lives.

We find ourselves on that peculiar charm of English scenery, a green common, divided by the road; the right side fringed by hedgerows and trees, – and terminated by a double avenue of noble oaks; the left, prettier still, dappled by bright pools of water, and islands of cottages and cottage gardens and sinking gradually down to cornfields and meadows and an old farm-house, with pointed roofs and clustered chimneys looking out from its blooming orchard backed by woody hills.

In her own day, Miss Mitford was known for a much wider range of writing than *Our Village*. In 1836, when she was fifty, she visited London and so many wished to meet this rosy-cheeked, bustling spinster that she had to refuse thirty dinner engagements. On this occasion she had come to meet a poet, Elizabeth Barrett, then thirty and unknown beyond her close friends. Miss Mitford's fame at that time was founded on the success of productions of her plays, *Rienzi* and *Julian*, on her poetry and literary criticism, and on the five volumes of *Village Sketches* published between 1824 and 1832.

Mary Russell Mitford first came to live in Berkshire when she was four years old. She later described her father as having 'every manly and generous quality, except that which is so necessary in the workaday world – the homely quality called prudence'. Dr Mitford, of aristocratic family but modest means, married an heiress, Miss Russell, and promptly gambled away her wealth. The family sold their most valued possessions and moved to Southampton Street in Reading, where Dr Mitford set up in practice. Some 'modest-looking dwelling houses, old-fashioned inns and the spire of the church of St Giles high above the roofs' remain today, though the street is noisier. The four-year-old only child later wrote that she remembered the garden of the house and 'a certain dell on the Bristol Road to which I used to resort for primroses'.

Moderate success did not satisfy Dr Mitford and he moved to a large house in Lyme Regis. However, his gambling again caused the family to sell up, leave 'in a sort of tilted cart without springs' and hide in London. On Mary's tenth birthday Dr Mitford decided to mend the family fortunes by investing in a lottery ticket. Amazingly the gamble succeeded; Mary chose the numbers 2224 and, although the ticket was torn, would not change her mind because they added up to her new age. She won twenty thousand pounds, a fortune indeed in 1795. This opulence resulted in a move back to Reading and a new redbrick house in the London Road, which was then on the edge of the country. The house, with its veranda in front and its long garden behind, is the home of a dental practice, as two centuries ago it housed Dr Mitford's dispensary.

London Road did not remain Mary's home for long; she attended the Abbey School for four years, during its time in London, and by 1802, when her formal lessons ended, her home was an Elizabethan farmhouse in Grazeley; it had 'ornamental panelling, oriel windows and a great oaken staircase' and was set in seventy acres of fields. Dr Mitford at first intended to restore Grazeley Court, but decided to pull down the old house and build an imposing new one, to be called Bertram House. Unfortunately, the doctor was unaware of the cost of such an undertaking. By now, the daughter was largely supporting the family with her writing; money continued to be lost in Dr Mitford's useless speculations and by 1820 the family had to leave Bertram House, which was later demolished. They moved to the cottage in Three Mile Cross, which was much visited in her day and now has a plaque in her honour. In a letter dated April 1820, just after the move, Mary wrote sadly that the rooms were 'a series of closets, the largest of which may be eight feet square, which they call parlours and kitchens and pantries,' and 'Behind is a garden about the size of a good drawing room, with an arbour which is a complete sentry box of privet.' But she adds 'It is within reach of my dear old walks'. Later she made a showpiece of the garden; her 'flowery domain' was in fact an acre. One day she heard that 'half the parish had mounted on a hayrick close by to look at the garden', so when some workmen had left, she climbed their ladder to take a view herself. What she saw was:

> Masses of the Siberian larkspur, and sweet Williams, mostly double, the still brighter new larkspur [Delphinium chiensis] *rich as an oriental butterfly* – such a size and such a blue! amongst roses in millions, with blue and white Canterbury

bells, and the white foxglove and the variegated monkshood, the carmine pea, in its stalwart beauty, the nemophila, like the sky above its head, the new erysimum with its gay orange tufts, and fuchsias, zinnias, salvias, geraniums beyond compt.

In Three Mile Cross many of the buildings described in *Our Village* are kept as close to their original form as possible. The 'flower-decked village Inn', the Swan, is there, as is the village shop; the bakery cottage, complete with ovens, is now a florist's. Opposite, some things have changed: where the cobbler worked and carters drove their fully laden wagons, today's motorists drive into bright buildings for petrol – yet, in their busy concern for trade or pleasure, they mimic those carters Miss Mitford observed many years ago.

Miss Mitford's last move was to Swallowfield in 1851; so many repairs to the Three Mile Cross house were needed a smaller cottage was found. She writes with regret at leaving all her homes in Berkshire but, always cheerful, is soon happy in her new setting. Of her move to Swallowfield she says:

I walked from the one cottage to the other in an Autumn evening. Here I am now in this prettiest village, in the cosiest of all snug cabins; a trim cottage garden, divided by a hawthorn hedge from a little field guarded by grand old trees; a cheerful glimpse of high road in front, just to hint that there is such a thing as a peopled world; on either side the deep silent woody lanes, that form the distinctive character of English scenery.

The Mitfords, Three Mile Cross.

This cottage, too, remains; it has been extended and its setting is less peaceful, but much is the same.

In spite of Dr Mitford's improvidence, his wife and daughter continued to admire him throughout their life together and lovingly faced each upheaval. He was a doting father, who included his child in many exciting activities and jaunts. He took her education seriously; he had a fine library and, to please him, Mary learned quickly. Mrs Mitford, writing to her husband, said that Mary, at her little desk with her great dictionary, was hard at her studies: 'Her little spirits are all abroad to obtain the prize, sometimes hoping, sometimes desponding.'

She did win prizes at school and in 1802, aged fourteen, writes home: 'I am glad my sweet mamma agrees with me as regards to Dryden, I never liked him as well as Pope.' Her teacher, Miss Rowden, knew only Pope's *Virgil* so could not judge; she adds: 'After I have read Pope's *Odyssey*, I think I shall read Ovid's *Metamorphoses*, which are very beautiful.'

Such was her cleverness, she taught herself Latin so she could read the originals. She was taken to the theatre and her passion for drama soon equalled that of Miss Rowden, although their pleasures differed: 'hers was a critical, mine a childish enjoyment; she loved fine acting, I loved the play.' She saw John Kemble and Mrs Siddons in *Macbeth*, *Coriolanus*, *Hamlet* and many more plays by Shakespeare and other playwrights.

The Mitford household had cultured friends whose experience was also an influence – Dr Valpy, Headmaster of Reading School, for example, and the St Quintins, French nobles whose property was lost in the Revolution. The intellectual Monsieur St Quintin became French master at the Abbey School and drew émigré families round him. Mary Mitford reports that at supper parties 'the conversation, music, games, manners and cookery were studiously and decidedly French; Grétry took the place of Mozart, Racine of Shakespeare; omelettes, champagne and *eau sucre* excluded sand-wiches, oysters and porter.' Dr Mitford's hope that his daughter would be musical was given up as she read Voltaire and Molière when she should have been practising piano or harp; she laughed so much at *Le Bourgeois Gentilhomme* that she did not hear approaching footsteps.

Another friend was William Cobbett; Mary, in her twenties, referred to him in one of her odes; Dr Mitford praised Cobbett's political ideals but Mary shared his love of rural scenery and ways with animals. The friend who became her most valued mentor was Sir William Elford. He was impressed by poems her father showed him and met Mary in 1810; for thirty years they exchanged letters, books and visits. He was courteous and had a great love of literature and art, she, fifty years younger, was lively and keen to share the joy she found in books. Writing in 1820 of *Much Ado About Nothing*, she claims that Beatrice is her standard of female wit; she is 'so lively, so clever, so unaffected and so warmhearted'; she adds 'Benedick is not quite equal to her; Shakespeare saw through nature, and knew which sex to make the cleverest. There's a challenge for you! Will you take up the glove?' Sir William visited Bertram House early in their friendship; Mary was afraid she would seem a 'plain, awkward, blushing thing' when they met, despite her 'wonderful boldness on paper'. They continued to write frequent letters until 1835, when Sir William Elford was over ninety, so she need not have worried.

By daily letter-writing, Mary Mitford kept in touch with valued friends such as the Reverend William Harness, the artist BR Haydon and invalid poet Elizabeth Barrett. In 1913 four hundred and thirty letters from Miss Barrett to Miss Mitford were sold at Sotheby's; even more were sent in the other direction. Over one thousand of Mary Mitford's letters in manuscript form still exist. By their exchange, literary experience and views could be circulated and problems or joys shared. The exchange of letters between Miss Mitford and Miss Barrett between 1836 and 1846, when most were written, shows them both coping with a widower 'of a difficult temper', but both gaining from the sharing of pleasures, actual or imagined. Elizabeth Barrett writes 'Thank you for your kind words about my verses – and for letting me see your garden in your words about it. You used it as a painter's palette did you not? I would choose the broad sky for my flight and the high mountains for my prospect.' Her physically restricted life in London contrasts with her dreams, and also with the country air and energetic pursuits enjoyed by Mary Mitford.

Walking was always a pleasure; a letter to Sir William Elford in 1812 shows that Mary had 'just returned from one of those field rambles which in the first balmy days of spring are so enchanting.' She tells of 'tall hedgerows, abounding in timber, strewn like a carpet with white violets, primroses and oxslips' and adds 'occasionally you catch a view of the soft valleys, the village churches and the fine houses which distinguish this part of Berkshire'. She often walked along the old drover's road, Woodcock Lane, and found a favourite place to sit and compose.

In that very lane am I writing on this sultry June day, luxuriating in the shade, the verdure, the fragrance of hayfield and beanfield, and the absence of any noise except the song of birds and the whir of a thousand forms of insect life so often heard among the general hush of a summer noon.

Woodcock Lane is shown in a Berkshire County Street Atlas as a footpath running beside the A33 Swallowfield bypass; the noises heard now are not from birds and insects! Many other favourite places Mary Mitford wrote about have, however, remained unspoiled. There are still fritillary fields by the Loddon off Chequer Lane, and the six-mile walk a friend led her 'on foot!', to find buckbean flowers, can be followed on footpaths and, as in her day, uses 'delicious lanes walled by honeysuckle hedges', passes 'the Loddon with its floating water-lilies', crosses woodlands at Barkham to the heath which is 'pink and purple with the flowers'.

Many fine old houses that Mary Mitford visited are familiar to walkers today. Several footpaths pass Ufton Court, for example; they weave through its woods and, beyond, give views of the Kennet Valley. Miss Mitford came this way to admire the 'fine proportion of the lofty and spacious apartments, the rich mouldings of the ceilings, and the carved chimney-pieces'; she also liked to walk in the grounds.

Among eminent visitors to the area, Queen Victoria and Prince Albert, on their way back to Windsor after staying with the Duke of Wellington at Stratfield Saye, were to pass near Three Mile Cross. Miss Mitford wanted all the two hundred and ninety village children to see the Queen, so she arranged that 'waggons lent by the kind farmers' should take them to Swallowfield Lane. The position was chosen well; the royal party paused there to bid farewell to the Duke and all had a good view and then returned to a spread of cakes, sandwiches and ale. 'All this seems little enough; but the ecstasy of the children made it much,' she told Miss Barrett.

All of the published work of Mary Mitford was written in Berkshire. The most famous, *Our Village*, appeared in 1824 and ran to three editions in its first year; further volumes of *Village Sketches* followed between 1826 and 1832. Her first play to be performed was *Julian*, with renowned William Macready as the principal character. In November 1826, *Foscari* with Charles Kemble was yet more successful, and in 1828 at Drury Lane *Rienzi* drew large audiences for a hundred days, a most unusual event in those times. Praise from such eminent female writers as Maria Edgeworth particularly pleased Miss Mitford, but she found working for the theatre meant frequent trips to London and, with her mother's health failing, she decided to revert to subjects nearer home. In *Belford Regis*, published in 1835, she depicts the events, characters and customs of the market town of Reading. The book is packed with history and anecdote, and its author liked it best of all her writing. She claims the characters 'are pure fiction' but admits she has 'stolen some touches of local scenery from the town that comes so frequently before my eyes'. She began to draw some more extended portraits. For example, prosperous butcher Steven Lane, with his great shop in the Butts, is large like his shop: 'when he walks he overfills the pavement, chairs crack under him and floors tremble'; he is large, too, in reputation: 'a leader of the opulent trades-people both socially and politically'. It is hard to believe she did not have a model in mind as she described Steven Lane.

Mary Mitford's fame grew abroad; her plays were produced overseas, and in 1841 in Philadelphia, USA, an edition of her collected works was published. Later works included *Recollections of a Literary Life* and *Country Stories*. Many of her letters were edited by Reverend AG L'Estrange and were published in 1870 in three volumes, as *The Life of Mary Russell Mitford*; these letters, perhaps more than her books, reveal a clever and indomitable woman, and are a lively record of local life a century and a half ago.

In 1852, returning from a visit to Lady Russell of Swallowfield Park, Miss Mitford was thrown from her pony-chaise; no bones were broken but she was much bruised and shaken. Typically, she wrote to a friend: 'the two parts of me that are quite uninjured are my head and my right hand'; these she continued to use, until her death in 1855. She lies in quiet Swallowfield churchyard, near the fields and wildlife about which she wrote with such dedication.

MARY RUSSELL MITFORD – WALK 4

WALK 4

A MARY RUSSELL MITFORD WALK OF EIGHT MILES, FROM THREE MILE CROSS

Ordnance Survey Landranger Sheet 175
START POINT: grid reference 713676

THIS WALK VISITS much of the Berkshire that Mary Russell Mitford lived and walked in. Although, as you are soon made aware, some of her favourite spots are now spoiled by traffic noise, the middle section of this walk goes through country almost as quiet as it was in her day.

Begin from Three Mile Cross, south of M4 Junction 11, on the outskirts of Reading. Turn left into the Old Basingstoke Road and park in Grazeley Road, first right after two garages.

First walk back to the main road and on the opposite side, to the right, find 'The Mitfords'; in this cottage, as the plaque on it shows, Miss Mitford lived and wrote from 1820 to 1851. The house, restored and retaining its well in the forecourt, is now owned by Colwood House. Near by are shops that were here when *Our Village* was written; some of the present proprietors are descended from those who traded here in the 1800s. On the wall of the Swan Inn is a marble profile of Mary Mitford.

To trace the route Miss Mitford probably took when she set out to walk from Three Mile Cross to her new home three miles away in Swallowfield, return to Grazeley Road, walk to the end and veer left to Woodcock Lane. It now skirts the A33 Swallowfield bypass; in its quieter days, Miss Mitford came here to sit in the sun among the primroses and write for hours. Follow the track ahead, trying to ignore the traffic noise; above, on the left, is where Dr Mitford built Bertram House. Continue ahead for about a mile, crossing with care over a turning from the bypass, and, after about a half a mile, climb to cross the Beech Hill Road.

Turn left up the hill, then shortly right at 'Yaffles', on a path that returns to Woodcock Lane.

Continue south-east for about half a mile then, at a footpath sign by some barns, turn left on a tarmac lane and, at the next junction, right toward Swallowfield, passing across the River Loddon, then go left into Barge Lane. This road is joined by Spring Lane from the right; where these lanes join, is the house in which Miss Mitford spent her last years. Now much extended, with lovely gardens and views, it remains secluded.

To reach Miss Mitford's burial place, at Swallowfield Church, continue along Barge Lane and, at the Old Basingstoke Road, walk left a few yards then cross into Charlton Lane. When this joins Trowse's Lane, walk a few yards right and cross into a track on the left. Soon turn right into a hedged path and go ahead, ignoring a path sign halfway along. Crossing two stiles and keeping to the hedge on the right, reach Part Lane then follow the clearly defined path opposite by stiles and footbridges over the Broadwater to Church Road. All Saints Church is a short way on the left; to find Mary Russell Mitford's grave, pass right of the church and walk to the far side of the churchyard. A simple but solid cross is inscribed with her name; she lies close to the park where she spent many happy hours.

Enter the park by the kissing gate and walk down to the bridge; this is where Miss Mitford's carriage was upset in 1852. Walk left across the bridge, and ahead to a gate and reach the Street. Here turn right past the Village Hall and, at the B3349, right again; pass the Mill House then turn right on a footpath that passes Sheepbridge Court Farm. Follow this round slightly to the right to a footpath sign; here turn left through small paddocks and a lane to the major road ahead.

Cross the road with care to a stile; follow this path across two small fields, then turn left into another lane. Where this joins Clares Green Road, walk right and at the bend turn right and after a few yards at a footpath sign (opposite), enter a track, then a path a little to the left to reach a stile, which you cross. Walk ahead through two fields keeping near the right-hand hedge. After a stile at the bottom of the slope, turn left with hedge now on your left to another stile and the main road at Three Mile Cross again.

Grazeley Road is opposite.

THOMAS HUGHES, 1822–1896

I know only two English neighbourhoods thoroughly, and in each, within a circle of five miles, there is enough of interest and beauty to last any reasonable man his life.

SO WRITES THOMAS Hughes in *Tom Brown's Schooldays*. He continues:

All I say is, you don't know your own lanes and woods and fields. Though you may be chock full of science, not one in twenty of you know where to find the wood-sorrel or bee-orchis, which grow in the next wood, or on the down three miles off, or what the bog-bean and wood-sage are good for. And as for the country legends...the place where the last skirmish was fought in the civil wars, where the last parish butts stood...they're gone out of date altogether.

THOMAS HUGHES

Thomas Hughes wrote *Tom Brown's Schooldays* in 1856, when his son, then eight, was leaving home for his first school. Hughes, wondering what advice he could give, felt a mainly autobiographical story based on his own schooldays might be helpful and also of general interest. The 'two English neighbourhoods' Hughes refers to are both in Berkshire, or were when he lived in them. He was born in Uffington in The Vale of the White Horse, then, from the age of eleven, lived with his family in Donnington, near Newbury, when he was not away at school. Although he says there are many areas of the country that have their own special attractions, 'none can be richer than the one I am speaking of, and going to introduce you to very particularly'.

This Hughes does, in both *Tom Brown's School Days* and *The Scouring of the White Horse*, and now when we walk on the downs or in the valleys, we can share his early memories, as well as the history he compiled on later visits when he both explored and studied the countryside he loved.

Thomas Hughes knew Uffington Rectory as a child; his grandmother, born Mary Ann Watts, was energetic and clever and had a strong influence on her son and all his eight children. Her husband, father, grandfather and great-grandfather had all, in turn, been vicars of Uffington and she passed down a love of the village and the nearby countryside to the younger family members. She also had literary friends, including Walter Scott, so it is no surprise that her grandson took easily to writing later in life.

Thomas also saw writing in progress in his father's study. John Hughes composed essays and papers on history and travel; Mary Russell Mitford's opinion of his work was indeed high! She praised his accurate research and his ability to catch the reader's attention and added: 'Legend for legend, tale for tale, wisdom for wisdom, song for song and jest for jest, he was a match for Geoffrey Chaucer.'

John Hughes, as Squire Brown in *Tom Brown's Schooldays*, also had 'true popular sympathies', playing cricket and football all his life with his villagers; he also praised them for their 'industry', which he saw as a true Christian duty. Son, Thomas, shared his father's attitudes saying, 'Nothing pleased me so much as playing with the village children.' His mother's care of those around them also impressed the boy; portrayed as the squire's wife in his writing, she 'dealt out calico shirts, and smock frocks, and comforting drinks to the old folks with the "rheumatiz", and good counsel to all; and kept the coal and clothes clubs going for yule-tide'.

In *Tom Brown's Schooldays*, the three-year-old Tom also saw the mummers at Christmas, 'repeating in true sing-song vernacular the legend of St George and his fight'. As Tom grew, he became better acquainted with the old festivals and the countryside where they flourished. A companion on many of his expeditions was 'old Benjy'; at seventy, retired and devoted to the family, he was 'a cheery, humorous, kind-hearted old man, full of sixty years of vale gossip'. Benjy took Tom to the annual village 'veast' day, which was thought to celebrate the ancient founding of the church and the festival of its patron saint. He introduced Tom to fishing, riding and other country activities.

When Thomas Hughes was eight, he and his elder brother George were sent to school in Twyford, near Winchester; unusually for 1830, prizes were given for gymnastics, and the learning by heart of poetry was encouraged. In a later essay Hughes wrote: 'We were allowed to choose our own poets and I always chose Scott from family tradition and in this way learned the whole of *The Lady of the Lake* and most of the *Lay of the Last Minstrel* and *Marmion*.'

As recorded in *Tom Brown's Schooldays*, when the boys returned home for holidays they made their own amusements 'within a walk or ride of home'. 'And so we got to know the country folk, and their ways and songs and stories by heart; and went over the fields, and woods, and hills, again and again, till we made friends of them all. '

The White Horse, cut in the chalk of the downs, imposed its presence on those who lived in the Vale. During their extensive walks along the Ridgeway the boys would have seen Uffington Castle, 'Wayland Smith's cave', and Ashdown House and Park. In the Vale to the east they could discover the Blowing Stone and listen to strange stories about it. Though some of Hughes's factual detail must be revised in view of the recent research that is discussed later, a wealth of early history in the Uffington area would have been as impressive in 1833 as it is today. Map-making was in progress in the 1850s:

> There is always a breeze in the 'camp', as it is called; and here it lies, just as the Romans left it, except that cairn on the east side left by Her Majesty's corps of Sappers and Miners the other day, when they and the Engineer officer had finished their sojourn there and their surveys for the Ordnance map of Berkshire.

When Thomas Hughes was eleven, his grandfather died and his father bought Donnington Priory, close to Donnington Castle. The latter was still, in spite of the damage suffered in the civil war, an impressive sight and provided the Hughes family with another 'neighbourhood' rich in history and natural beauty to explore and enjoy. In 1833 Thomas Hughes attended Rugby School and in 1842 he entered Oriel College, Oxford, so it was in the long vacations that he could share family life in Donnington.

From 1842, when he first met seventeen-year-old Frances Ford, who was later to become his wife, he gained another companion for his walks. A diary kept by Hughes recorded their 'long rambles together by the Old Castle'. The Ford parents thought the couple too young to know their own minds, so insisted on a separation, which the lovers bore with patience. To make himself worthy of her, he 'lived decently and took his degree as soon as possible without coaching'. A few days after his final examinations in May 1845, Tom's journal records, 'I have heard such news dear Fanny'. He explains that her father had written to his father 'as if he had made up his mind *to the worst,*' and says that her mother, in another letter, 'talks calmly of our engagement'. He continues: 'Can such things be? I think after this you *must* be allowed to come to Donnington at Christmas and then! and then!! and then!!! but I won't anticipate.'

The visit was allowed, but it was another two years before they were wed. The years were not wasted, though; during his time in Donnington, Hughes read avidly and encouraged Frances to share his love of the literature of Dickens, Austen, Pope and, of course, Scott. His journal mentions the historical and religious works he read, especially Dr Arnold's *Sermons on Christian Life*, given to him by his Rugby tutor when he left Oriel.

Hughes gave serious thought to his choice of career; although the life of a country clergyman appealed, he decided to become a barrister: 'May God enable me to do my duty in it', he noted in his journal. The poverty he saw in the back streets of London shocked a young man used to ordered life in a country village. He earned his first legal fee in 1846 and by 1848 he had married Frances, been called to the Bar and was also, with Charles Kingsley and others, developing a Christian Socialism Movement. To promote fair treatment for workers, he helped set up trade unions and co-operatives and developed legal frameworks for these. Keen to show that education is not just for the wealthy, Hughes and Kingsley in 1854 set up the Working Men's College; general study,

Tom Brown's School Museum and St Mary's Church, Uffington.

sport and even cultural excursions were on its curriculum.

Alongside these activities, Kingsley and others had written books, which aimed to further Christian Socialist ideas. Little had been written for children that was both jolly and of sound moral tone. So Thomas Hughes showed *Tom Brown's Schooldays* to Alexander Macmillan, who readily agreed to publish it. When Kingsley tried to 'push' the book to help his friend he discovered that everyone seemed to have found it and claimed it was 'the jolliest book ever read'. Popular then because it was the first book of its kind, with 'actual knowledge of boys' and written in their lively slang, it is valuable reading now for walkers because its early chapters depict so vividly White Horse Hill and the villages in the Vale below it, with the cottages 'in nooks and corners by shadowy lanes and footpaths'. Tom Brown used footpaths and took new boy Arthur on 'some good long walks'. However, when the latter praised his native Devon, Tom jealously stood up for 'the clear chalk streams, and the emerald meadows and great elms and willows of the dear old Royal county'. And so should we!

Hughes wrote the second book that gives a lively picture of the Vale, its downs and customs, *The Scouring of the White Horse*, at the request of the committee that organised the Scouring of 1857 and the Pastime to go with it. The book is in fictional form with the sub-title, *The Long Vacation Ramble of a London Clerk*. The author was present at the events and also carried out careful research but, by allowing his young clerk to record facts and views gleaned from both learned and rustic participants, Hughes is able to include documents, dialect and even a love story.

In 1855 Hughes, with Fanny and the two children, had visited his brother John at Longcot Rectory. An outing to White Horse Hill, three miles away, with steep climbs and tales of dragons, so pleased the children that Hughes's enthusiasm for writing about its history was rekindled. Only a little of the wealth of material in *The Scouring of the White Horse* can be given here but a report in the *Reading Mercury* of May 1870 sets the scene:

The ceremony of scowering and cleansing that noble monument of Saxon antiquity, the White Horse, was celebrated on Whit-Monday, with great joyous festivity. Besides the customary horse-racing, foot-races, etc. many uncommon rural diversions and feats of activity were exhibited to a greater number of spectators than assembled on any former occasion. Upwards of thirty thousand persons were present, and amongst them most of the nobility and gentry of this and the neighbouring counties; and the whole was concluded without any material accident.

The White Horse is now known to be much older than Saxon. The Tom Brown's School Museum in Uffington records how in 1994 the Oxford Archaeological Unit used the technique known as Optical Stimulated Luminescence, which gives the approximate date of the last exposure to sunlight of the buried soil. Samples taken from the Horse now suggest that it was created in the Late Bronze Age, around 1000 BC, meaning it is by far the oldest-known chalk hill carving.

The design of the White Horse is stylised, with a slender body and beaked jaw, like the horses seen on early Iron Age coins. HJ Pye, Farringdon poet laureate in the late 1700s, describes it:

> Carved rudely on the pendent soil is seen
> The snow-white courser stretching o'er the green.

Illustrations by Richard Doyle in the 1859 edition of Hughes's book also show its elongated shape. That it can best be seen at some distance from the country north of the Ridgeway shows its importance, and the cleansing with feasting and sport held every seven years or so suggests a periodic religious festival. It remains, however, a figure of legend. The 1857 Pastime, which Hughes records in such detail, was the last to be held on such a scale. The hand-bill that announced this two-day fête lists the events and prizes:

> Backsword play…Old gamesters – £8
> Young gamesters – £4
> Wrestling…Old gamesters – £5
> Young Gamesters – £4
> A jingling match, Foot races, Hurdle races, Races of cart-horses in Thill harness [for a new set of harness], Donkey race [for a flitch of bacon], Climbing pole [for a leg of mutton], Races down 'The Manger' [for cheeses], A pig turned out on the Downs to be won by the catcher.

Most controversial was back-swording, fought with sticks, disapproved of by some but keenly contested between men from 'Barkshire, Zummerztshire and Wiltshire'. The entertainment tents were erected and the events took place in the Iron Age Hill Fort, Uffington Castle, or near by and most of the participants walked up to the arena from their villages in the Vale. After reading *The Scouring of the White Horse*, a walk on the Ridgeway near Uffington becomes a new experience.

Thomas Hughes wrote six more books during his later years. He became a Member of Parliament for Lambeth in 1865 and could therefore introduce bills for working men's rights himself. In 1868 his constituency was Frome. He was made Queen's Counsel in 1869 and, in 1885, Recorder of Chester. A change of direction in 1880 saw him founding an English Colony, named Rugby, in the United States. Though ideals of co-operation governed the venture, it failed partly because the woodland in which it was set was unsuitable for farming. Thomas Hughes's mother moved there, to live in a house built for her called 'Uffington', and his brother Hastings also made his home in America. Hughes is now honoured there by an association that has restored the church, library, school and houses, and opens them to the public.

When Thomas Hughes moved to Chester, he had a house built which he also named Uffington. When he died in 1896, his wife Frances resisted talk of a Memoir for him, but he has not been ignored by later biographers. In Uffington Church there is a plaque with his portrait, the village hosts the Thomas Hughes Memorial Hall, and the Tom Brown's School Museum is housed in the small schoolhouse he knew as a boy. For most, the books he wrote to celebrate the 'Royal County', especially the wild rural beauty, the customs, and the history of its western reaches, are his strongest claim to our interest.

THOMAS HUGHES – WALK 5

THIS WALK BEGINS in Uffington, where Thomas Hughes was born, and climbs the dramatic stretches of downs and Ridgeway that, after careful research and with much fondness, Hughes featured in his writing. It is a nine-mile walk (a shorter one could hardly do justice to such magnificent scenery), but if you would prefer something shorter, make use of the car parks near the White Horse and on the Ridgeway, as shown on the map. In addition, a stroll in Uffington, taking in the places referred to below, would be worthwhile. Uffington lies north of the B4507, about eight miles west of Wantage.

Begin the walk from the Thomas Hughes Memorial Hall and walk slightly to the right into Broad Street. Many of the older cottages on the right are built of chalkstone and are thatched, much as when Thomas Hughes saw them as a boy. On the right just before St Mary's Church, the Primary School was built for girls, in 1851, on the site of an old farmhouse that had been the birthplace of Hughes in 1822. As a child, Thomas knew an older vicarage, in which his grandparents lived, and the boy's school, further along the road, which now houses Tom Brown's School Museum. This small chalk building, reached by following the sarsen stone path

WALK 5

A THOMAS HUGHES WALK OF NINE MILES FROM UFFINGTON, WHICH REFERS ALSO TO JOHN BETJEMAN AND WALTER SCOTT

Ordnance Survey Landranger Sheet 174
START POINT: grid reference 306894

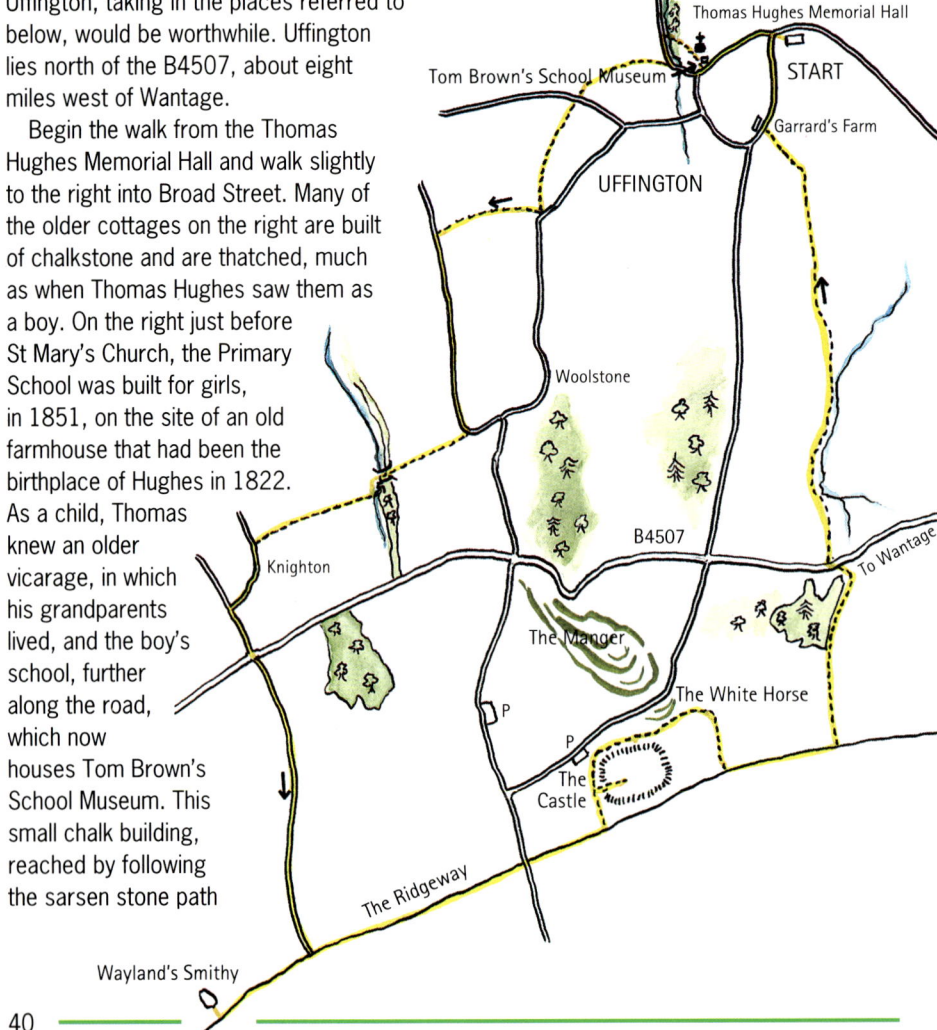

40

THOMAS HUGHES – WALK 5

on the right-hand verge, was the Thomas Saunders School House that is described in *Tom Brown's Schooldays*. The Museum is open on weekend afternoons from Easter until the end of October.

In the imposing St Mary's Church look for a fine plaque to T Hughes, QC; his grandfather's service as vicar is also recorded. John Betjeman, who was churchwarden in the 1930s, described St Mary's, Uffington as

> *Of purest Early English, tall and pale,*
> *To tourists 'Cathedral of the Vale'*
> *To us, the Church.*

To continue, walk past the little museum, take the path on the left side of the churchyard and the stile at the far end. Keep to the left of the field, cross a fence and a footbridge. This spans the small stream where old Benjy, in *Tom Brown's Schooldays*, brought Tom to see sticklebacks. Continue the walk they took to the Feast Day Revels by passing a willow and walking to a road. Benjy also visited the cottage opposite, which was then an alehouse.

Walk left along the road beside the stream and, as the road bears left, turn right into Grounds Farm drive and, after a bungalow, right over a stile. Ignore paths ahead that pass a barn in the middle of the field, but keep left to follow the left edge of the field and, after passing buildings on your left, take a footbridge and stile left, on to a road.

Cross the road and stile opposite, take the footpath straight ahead to a metal gate and go through this. Bear hard left to cross a stile and footbridge and walk to the far corner of the field ahead and a road. Immediately turn right, between a cottage and small stream, cross a stile, go through a paddock and over two stiles, follow the right edge of the field to a footbridge, cross this then continue straight across the next field to a road.

Turn left into this quiet lane, Marsh Way, and walk for about half a mile to where it bears sharply left by Upper Farm. Here follow the footpath sign to the right, cross two fields using gate and stile. The White Horse may be glimpsed over trees to the left. A stile ahead leads to an old track, called Hardwell Lane; enter this and after about five yards, turn right across a footbridge. Walk left to the field edge then, keeping the hedge on your left, walk ahead through two fields using a metal gate. Ignore a stile on the left but cross one ahead, where the fields end, to reach a lane in Knighton.

Turn left up the hill and left again to reach the main road, the B4507, which you cross. The narrow lane opposite leads up to the Ridgeway; it is a steep climb, a mile long, so pause often to look back at the view, which gets more spectacular the higher you go. Recall also that it was up Woolstone Hill or Blowingstone Hill that thousands climbed, with their stalls and wares, to be a part of the 1857 Pastime, recorded in *The Scouring of the White Horse*.

At the Ridgeway, you can see Wayland's Smithy by walking right for about a quarter of a mile; this is the ancient burial chamber included in their writing by both Hughes and Sir Walter Scott.

To continue the walk to the Iron Age Hill Fort, Uffington Castle, and the White Horse, turn back and follow the Ridgeway eastwards. As you climb to the site of the 'castle', whose history runs back to at least 500 BC, find a stile on the left by which you can reach the earthworks and, over to their right, the White Horse. Imagine, in the flat centre of the fort, tents and booths crowded with 'thirty thousand persons', 'amongst them most of the nobility and gentry of this and the neighbouring counties', then look into the valley to see the curves of the Manger, down which cheeses were raced. Also notice the small Dragon's Hill, to the right of it. Walk over the downs, right, to see the White Horse, kept scoured in the chalk for 3,000 years; from above, its spreading shape is less easy to appreciate than when seen at a distance.

To continue, return to The Ridgeway and walk east for about a quarter of a mile, then take a wide grassy footpath on the left, which descends sharply. Keeping a small wood on your left, cross stiles on the way, and from the left corner of the bottom field reach the B4507, right of Britchcombe Farm.

Walk left along the road a few paces, then cross to a footpath on the right indicating, 'Uffington 1.25 miles'. Follow this path, with woods and stream on your right, through two fields; then turn left over a footbridge and stile and continue, with the stream and trees now on your left. Ignore one footbridge on the left but cross the next one, which is almost at the end of the field, then turn right through an area of newly planted trees, with the stream again on your right.

At the end of the field, ignoring a footbridge on the right, turn left over a stile and walk right, keeping fence and hedge on your right. Walk ahead to cross a double stile then cross a field slightly left to take a stile in the hedge. Now, keeping the hedge on your right, cross three fields by stiles, where they exist; after crossing a stile beyond some electricity or telegraph cables, turn diagonally left across a field to a stile at the road, which is High Street, Uffington. The house opposite, Garrard's Farm, is where John Betjeman, his wife and baby son, lived from 1934 to 1941.

To return to the Thomas Hughes Memorial Hall, walk right along the road.

ROBERT BRIDGES, 1844–1930

When men were all asleep the snow came flying
In large white flakes falling on the city brown
Stealthily and perpetually settling and loosely lying
Hushing the latest traffic of the drowsy town;

'LONDON SNOW' IS perhaps Robert Bridges' best-known poem; a great city is transformed by a new beauty and the poet's skill captures the scene so aptly that his words come to mind whenever winter brings such seasonal weather. At the time of writing, snow is falling on the Berkshire fields and woods beyond my windows, a scene described exactly by phrases from the poem such as 'Lazily and incessantly floating down and down', 'its uncompacted lightness', 'the white-mossed wonder'. Bridges' mastery of poetic form and close observation of the natural world combine to produce verse that enables a reader to share the wonder of the boys in the poem as they cry 'O look at the trees!'.

Robert Bridges lived in Yattendon, in Berkshire, for twenty-two years. During those years he produced a steady flow of lyrics, plays, narrative poetry and other literary papers. Yattendon, where wide stretches of downland slope to small woods and streams, gave him the quiet and order of village life and the wild beauty that he loved.

Born in Kent in 1844 into a prosperous family, Bridges was one of nine children. Many of his early memories were happy, but he also knew what it meant to grieve. His father died when he was eight, and two brothers and two sisters had died by the time he was thirty-two. Most sad was the loss of his youngest brother, Edward, who, too delicate for school life but a keen musician, visited Robert at Eton School to hear anthems in St George's Chapel, Windsor Castle, and to take trips on the Thames. Edward died at the age of twenty and Robert, writing later to his sister Frances, when he himself was a doctor, said: 'I am this evening in a state of dejection...I am surprised at reading Edward's letters to find that he had a much greater command of language than I remembered...I always think that the means taken to guard against his disease were sadly insufficient.'

This experience influenced his choice of career; when he left Oxford, he enrolled as a medical student at St Bartholomew's Hospital. Some early poetry has imagery that also echoes his prevailing mood.

The wood is bare: a river mist is steeping
The trees that winter's chill of life bereaves;
Only their stiffened boughs break silence, weeping
Over their fallen leaves...
Shorter Poems, Book I

While at Eton and Oxford, Bridges formed friendships, interests and some patterns of thinking that he was to develop later in life. In his Corpus Christi rooms, he entertained Gerard Manley Hopkins and Lionel Muirhead. Bridges was at a later stage of life responsible for publishing Hopkins's poetry; Muirhead, country gentleman and artist, was his close friend for sixty years. Bridges' main studies during school and college were the usual classics and philosophy, but he was aware, too, of the 1860s interest in science. His early love of music formed the basis of much future work; in 'Three Friends' he recalls slipping away at afternoon break to hear the Eton choir sing Early English church music in St George's Chapel. Hubert Parry tried out a new school organ with Bridges, who later wrote words for Parry's music. Bridges, in private, wrote poetry also but, as with his earliest music, discarded it later.

All through his life Bridges enjoyed outdoor activities; he rowed and played football for his Oxford college and frequently refers to walking. At fifteen he met Samuel Butler, who was to be his brother-in-law; they had at least 'one day's ramble together on the moors'. During the years of his medical work in London, he felt the need for open-air exercise and joined The Tramps, which was a rambling club 'whose members took long walks in the country on Sundays'. When in Seaford for a few days, he had 'a splendid sail and got drenched with salt water'; he also 'walked twenty-five miles and got wet to the skin with aerial showers'.

Bridges followed a medical career for thirteen years; after training he became house physician then assistant physician at the Hospital for Sick Children, Great Ormond Street, and at the Great Northern Hospital, in Holloway.

He had planned to retire in his forties so he could devote all his time to poetry and other literary work, but he was forced to break ties with medicine in 1881, when he suffered from such a severe pneumonia attack that return to strenuous hospital work was not advised. Travel in the warmth of Italy, with Lionel Muirhead, restored his energy, however. He walked and was able to make a four-hour ascent and decent of Vesuvius after a few months without feeling overtired.

The move to Yattendon was made in 1882. Alfred Waterhouse, architect and old friend, owned the Yattendon estate and having built a new family house, Yattendon Court, on the hill above the village, wished to let the Manor House. Bridges moved into this roomy eighteenth-century home with his widowed mother, and a settled and productive phase of his life began. The poet Henry Newbolt, who visited more than once, wrote: 'The pleasant old red-brick house with its rook-haunted garden had just the combination of beauty, simplicity and remoteness suitable to a poet of his Miltonic order.' 'The Sleeping Mansion' was a later poem by Bridges about this house.

Bridges' family circle grew, too. In 1884 he married Monica Waterhouse, eldest child of Alfred, and by 1892 daughters Elizabeth and Margaret and son, Edward, were born. Bridges clearly appreciated family life; his letters refer to visits made or activities enjoyed. Writing in 1897 to a guest who had stayed on a rainy weekend, he comments: 'Today has been lovely. I wish Sunday had been like it. We took the children out into the woods and gathered fir cones. You did not see any of our woods, or rather forests: which I now much regret as they are our chief attraction.'

The countryside, and its effect on those who live and work in it, forms the subject matter of much of Bridges' poetry, and he seeks to protect it. On another walk, he hears the sound of a tree being felled; the poet shares a sense of loss as the 'iron axe' 'hammered the iron heart of the oak.' The nearby trees seem to sense a loss so 'appalling'

As a hundred years of pride
Crashed, in the silence falling;
And the shadowy pine trees sighed.
Shorter Poems, Book IV

Country workers are seen as happy and healthy in their work and they are compared with those whose 'evil lot' is 'toil for gain' in city crowds. Out walking, the poet would come to a 'little hamlet' and see farming as rich satisfying work, the cattle 'Knee-deep in straw...'

twitching 'Sweet hay from crib and rack'. Inside a barn grain is being winnowed:

> *One turns the crank, one stoops to feed*
> *The hopper, lest it lack,*
> *One in the bushel scoops the seed,*
> *One stands to hold the sack.*
> Shorter Poems, Book V

The brown-armed labourers laughed 'because the wheat was clean and plump and good, / Pleasant to hand and eye,' Bridges ends the poem by stating that onlookers from the city toiled but produced little of such value.

Bridges invited visitors to share his delight in the countryside near Yattendon. 'The weather is delightful, and the country is looking at its best', he wrote to Lionel Muirhead in October 1887. He claims the trees are better than he had ever known them and adds: 'All is light golden browns and light greens, the skies every day are cloudless blue, and the air sharp and brisk.' Ideal walking weather, of course, and, as he said to George Sainsbury, who was coming to stay in November 1890, 'he did go to Church at 11.00 and at 6.15 on Sundays but that left the afternoons free for a walk unless you want to walk all day.'

Trains from London brought his guests to Pangbourne, six miles from Yattendon; sometimes a dog-cart was sent to meet them, but often they walked from the station. Later they could catch trains to Hampstead Norris, two miles from the house. These long distances were often walked by his friends. Writer Margaret Woods, said she had not been well; in his reply to her Bridges wrote: 'if you walk 16 miles a day you can't be so bad.'

Some of the most eminent literary figures of the period were visitors to Yattendon Manor House. Gerard Manley Hopkins stayed in August 1887. In 1884 Bridges had asked Hopkins to be his best man but he had been ill; by then in Dublin, working in a Jesuit Community, Hopkins could manage only a rare visit. Both poets had recently written poetic plays and gave each other copies for comment: the writing differed in style and subject matter, but their respect for each others' integrity and skill was considerable. In May 1889 Bridges was shocked to hear of his friend's death. All Hopkins's writing was unpublished at that time and by helping his family to sort his poetry, notes and letters, and to prepare them for publication, Bridges performed a valuable service to English literature.

William Butler Yeats was also invited to stay. Bridges wrote in March 1897: 'You will be received in the name of poet, and find others here besides myself who are friends of your work.' Yeats visited that year in March and was invited for 'a week's country air and retirement in the Summer'. They discussed current work, and Bridges' role as mentor to other writers was as significant as his own literary creation.

Bridges' poetry is full of precise descriptions of the natural world. He was a competent field botanist, as he reveals in 'The Idle Flowers'. Seventy-six wild plants are named; all are given their typical habitat. Plants 'Upon the marsh...' 'King-cup and Fleur-de-lys', 'With Comfrey, Water-mint, Loosestrife and Meadowsweet.'

> *And in the shady lanes*
> *Bold Arum's hood of green,*

Herb Robert, Violet,
Starwort and Celandine;

And by the dusty road
Bedstraw and Mullein tall,
With red Valerian
And Toadflax on the wall,

Walks also took the Bridges family further afield:

There is a hill beside the silver Thames,
Shady with birch and beech and odorous pine:
And brilliant underfoot with thousand gems
Steeply the thickets to his floods decline
Straight trees in every place
Their thick tops interlace,
And pendant branches trail their foliage fine
Upon his watery face.

When the children were old enough, the family bought a boat to use on the Thames. 'We had a good day on the river last week – and are going to try and get another tomorrow,' he wrote to Muirhead in August 1902.

Bridges took a full part in Yattendon life. Services in the Church of St Peter and St Paul were enriched by his efforts; he trained the choir from 1885 until 1894 and clearly enjoyed this. He wrote to Canon Dixon in August 1886: 'The choir goes on very well. Their performance is some-times admirable...Last Wednesday the chants were very difficult and they went without a hitch. It is nice to have one's work so well repaid.' To provide the choir with fine music, Bridges worked with his friend Harry Ellis Wooldridge to produce *The Yattendon Hymnal*, which was published in 1899. Wooldridge was responsible for the music, while Bridges edited and wrote words for twelve tunes. His wife, Monica, a skilled calligraphist, selected 'The Roman and Italic Type of Bishop Fell' for the words and Peter Walpergen's music type was used. Bridges explains in the preface that his chief object was to restore old melodies to use but his purpose was not antiquarian: 'the greater number of these old tunes are, without question, of an excellence which sets them above either the enhancement or the ruin of time'.

The Bridges family took part in music-making, in poetry readings and also in political events in Yattendon; they created an 'intellectual kindling and quickening in the place' according to the Waterhouse family. Even the rector of Yattendon Church, Henry Beeching, who married Bridges' niece, was a respected writer and critic; his poem 'Going Down Hill on a Bicycle' appears in many anthologies.

It was in Berkshire that much of Robert Bridges most significant work was produced; the first piece published during this time, was *Prometheus the Firegiver*, 'A mask in the Greek manner'. Bridges was present when boys of Newbury Grammar School performed it, and the classicist J Mackail reviewed it favourably, saying Bridges was 'a scholar who dares to be natural'. Eight poetic dramas in all were published, as well as *Poems* in 1884, *Shorter Poems* in two volumes 1890–4, *New Poems* in 1899 and *Now in Wintry Delights* in 1903. Further poems were written for journals. An edition of Hopkins's poetry, a study of Milton's prosody and *The Yattendon Hymnal* were among other works that reached publication. Critic JC Bailey wrote in 1893: 'Bridges' observant eye, nurtured by contemplation in a quiet village, makes country life delightful to us.'

During Bridges's years in Yattendon improvements were made to the manor house and its garden. By 1904, however, because of the ill health of both Monica and daughter Margaret, it was decided the family should move. 'I must take my invalids up to some hilltop', Robert Bridges wrote, and he cycled many miles looking for a suitable position. A new house, Chilswell, was built on ground at Boars Hill and a garden was laid out. 'I am really becoming a gardener and spend many hours propagating,' he wrote in a letter. Chilswell was in Berkshire in 1904, although it lies just a short walk over the fields from Oxford.

Bridges published more poetry, culminating in *The Testament of Beauty* in 1929, when he was eighty-three. By the Chilswell years, he had become a prominent public figure. In July 1913 he became Poet Laureate and he was awarded honorary degrees by many universities, including Cambridge, Oxford and Harvard, USA. He continued to surprise visitors with his energy; Virginia Woolf in 1926 described him as 'direct and spry, very quick in all his movements, racing me down the garden to look at pinks then to his library.'

Robert Bridges died in April 1930. Later, his son Edward was Chancellor of Reading University and as Bridges Hall is named after him there remains a strong link with the family in Berkshire. Words from *The Testament of Beauty* epitomise Robert Bridges' lifelong joy in nature and his energy. He climbed 'to where the path

Bridges' memorial cross, Church of St Peter and St Paul, Yattendon.

was narrowing and the company few,' then 'as any man may know who, rambling wide, hath turn'd, resting on some hill-top to view the plain he has left, and seen it now out-spread mapp'd at his feet, a landscape so by beauty estranged he scarce will [know] familiar haunts.'

Most walkers have shared that experience.

WALK 6

A ROBERT BRIDGES WALK OF FOUR AND A HALF MILES FROM YATTENDON

Ordnance Survey Landranger Sheet 174
START POINT: grid reference 552744

THIS WALK PASSES the Manor House in Yattendon, crosses fields to Saint Clement's Church, Ashampstead, and returns by Pinfold Lane and by woods to the Church of St Peter and St Paul and its churchyard in Yattendon.

Find Yattendon either by taking the B4009 south from Streatley and turning left from Hampstead Norreys, or by following minor roads north from the A4 at Woolhampton, between Newbury and Reading.

Park in the centre of Yattendon and, facing the Royal Oak, take a road to the left signposted Hampstead Norreys. To the right, as you walk, the Manor House can be glimpsed through the shrubs that border its garden. At a footpath sign on the right, take a diagonal path across the field; again, to the right, there are glimpses of the Manor House among its trees. It cannot be seen clearly from any public path.

At the hedge, turn right along a wide path and go left, after about two hundred yards, at a sign in the hedge that points left across the corner of the field on your left, to cross a stile in the hedge. Cross the field to a stile in the far left corner, then pass firs to another stile; cross the farm track and stile opposite and, keeping the hedge on the right, cross two more stiles and walk ahead across the field to reach a signpost. At this, turn right along a bridleway between trees and veer left when this becomes a hard farm track.

As Ashampstead Church comes into view, look for a stile on the right, use this and two more to enter the churchyard. The church, with thirteenth-century frescoes, rewards a visit. The Bridges family knew it well;

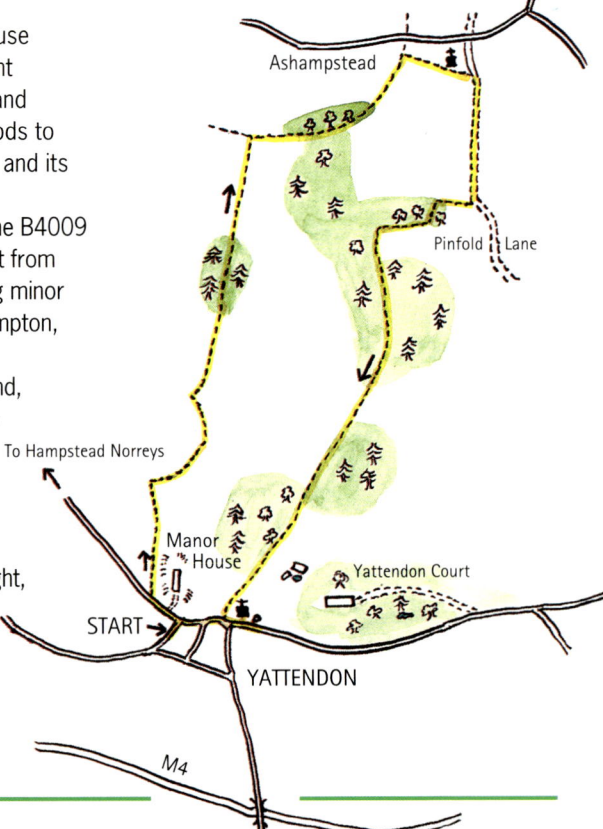

48

Alfred Waterhouse was paid £25 for having given 'valuable service' as consulting architect when sham plasterwork was removed to reveal the old oak roof.

The route Robert Bridges followed on his many rides to Oxford is likely to have taken him through Ashampstead; perhaps he used Pinfold Lane, the track you now follow. Turn right in front of the church and walk down a track to the left. At the bottom of the slope, take a right footpath across a field and turn a little left through trees to cross a stile; turn right then left, by a fenced plantation. Walk ahead and, as the path widens, see the roof and chimneys of the mock-Tudor Yattendon Court, built by Lord Edward Iliffe in 1925. This replaced the house built by Waterhouse in 1881, which Robert Bridges and his family visited so often. The group of buildings nearer the path is the home of the present Lord Iliffe.

Continue ahead to cross stiles and reach the road by Yattendon Church, or pass by a small gate into the churchyard. The large cross in front of the church was placed there by Bridges, in memory of his mother. He wrote to Mrs Manley Hopkins in December 1897: 'We had a beautifully sung service in our little village, and I have chosen a spot for her grave near the old yew tree, where strangely enough we found that in our old crowded little churchyard no one had ever been buried before.'

The cross still stands alone, but the yew has gone now. Inside the church, a tablet has been placed on the left wall, by the seat where Bridges sat as precentor. The poet wrote the dedication to his mother himself; added later were the words that state that his ashes and those of his wife, Monica, are buried near by. From the church, turn right to return to the start.

OSCAR WILDE, 1854–1900

'NO, NO,' HE said, and called a passing hansom. 'I never walk.'

Poet Wilfred Blunt recalls Oscar Wilde's words. They left a lunch party together and Blunt suggested they should walk, as they both lived just a short distance away, but Wilde was not to be persuaded. Later, in Paris, Wilde pointed to the sunlit boulevards and exclaimed: 'Ah, how all this outdoes the languishing beauty of the countryside. The solitude of the country stifles and crushes me...I am not really myself except in the midst of elegant crowds... I detest nature where man has not intervened with his artifice.'

Compared with other writers who have lived in Berkshire, Wilde seems to have taken few walks in the beauty of its countryside. Many aspects of his life and thinking, however, are contradictory. He did take walks in the woods at Goring when visitors came to stay, albeit remarking, when the path opened up for a short space, before winding round a blind corner ahead: 'There! that is as far as I ever want to see in life...I do not want to know what lies beyond the turning a few paces ahead.'

In Wilde's plays, it is unsophisticated characters who seem to be associated with things rural; in *Lady Windermere's*

OSCAR WILDE

Fan, when Lady Berwick wants to speak of scandal, she sends her daughter to the terrace to look at the sunset: 'Sweet girl! So devoted to sunsets! Shows such a refinement of feeling does it not? After all there is nothing like Nature, is there not?' In *The Importance of Being Ernest*, Jack describes his ward: '...Cecily is not a silly romantic girl, I am glad to say. She has a capital appetite, goes long walks, and pays no attention at all to her lessons.' When Gwendoline arrives, she asks 'Are there many interesting walks in the vicinity?' and Cecily assures her 'Oh! Yes! a great many. From the top of one of the hills quite close one can see five counties.' She could be speaking of a highpoint on the Ridgeway, just three miles from a Thames-side house where Wilde had spent a long summer. Gwendoline, who comes from London, replies 'Five counties! I don't think I would like that; I hate crowds.' She asks '...how anybody manages to exist in the country, if anybody who is anybody does', and adds 'The country always bores me to death.' The delightful acidity of their jibes arises, as often in Wilde, from misunderstandings that will heighten the comedy, and the contrasting views they hold suit the roles they have been given. Comparison of town and country is, however, a recurring theme.

Oscar Wilde was born in Dublin on 6 October 1854, to parents of outstanding ability. His father's skilled treatment of ear and eye diseases earned him a knighthood in 1864; some of the definitions in his medical textbooks are still in use today. He also wrote books on Ireland and about travel further afield. Lady Wilde published poetry, translations of French and German writers, and books of Irish folklore. Both Oscar and his brother, Willie, grew up among the most eminent in Irish society, attending the large parties given, and presided over, by their parents.

After excelling in classics at Trinity College, Dublin, where he won a gold medal for Greek, Wilde progressed to Oxford. Already an aesthete, he soon became a figure well-known for his wit and flamboyant clothes. He entertained generously in his rooms but, as a contemporary reports: 'Of course Wilde worked hard for the high academic honours he achieved at Oxford. He liked to pose as a dilettante trifling with his books; but I knew of his hours of assiduous and laborious reading, often into the small hours of the morning, after our pleasant symposia.'

Wilde left Oxford with a double first in Greats and the Newdigate Prize for his poem *Ravenna*, written after a tour of Greece and Italy in 1877.

Life in London began with much socialising and some writing. The plays *Vera* and *The Duchess of Padua* appeared and *Poems*, first published in 1881, had reached a fifth edition by early 1882. In that year too, Wilde embarked on a fifty-lecture tour of America. Speaking of the Aesthetic Movement, he was lionised and wrote 'Well its really wonderful...in Chicago, I lectured last Monday to 2500 people!'. The press, however, was not very kind; below headlines like 'The Sunflower Poet' or 'The Apostle of Beauty' came long reports of his appearance and short ones of his speeches.

In 1884 Oscar Wilde married Constance Lloyd. They leased No. 16, Tite Street, Chelsea, in London, and moved in after its costly redecoration. They had two sons, Cyril, born in 1885, and Vyvyan in 1886. In spite of later events, Oscar and Constance never lost their regard for each other and Wilde's love for his young sons is expressed in his work at that time, notably *The Happy Prince and Other Tales*, published in 1888.

A period of great creativity filled the next seven years or so. Wilde published stories and short novels, including *The Picture of Dorian Gray*, and he wrote the plays *Salomé*, *Lady Windemere's Fan*, *A Woman of No Importance*, *An Ideal Husband* and *The Importance of Being Ernest*. Some plays proved controversial: *Salomé* was banned in England because of its biblical subject matter, and so it was written in French and staged in France; the ban was removed in 1931. Others were received with acclaim, and Wilde had many friends from the theatre – great names such as Lily Langtry, Ellen Terry, Beerbohm Tree. The Wildes also knew, or were known by, most literary figures of the age, including WB Yeats, who was amazed that Oscar spoke in perfect sentences: 'as if he had written them all overnight with labour, yet all spontaneous.' Other associates, such as Lord Alfred Douglas, whose friendship with Wilde was to become a dominant feature in both their lives, posed a growing threat.

Berkshire was known to Wilde before 1895, when he was forced to stay in its largest town. He and his family joined weekend house-parties held by such leading Reading families as the Palmers, and he even toured their biscuit factory. Some of the characters in his plays were named after places in, or near, the Royal County. The cast list of *An Ideal Husband*, written at Goring, includes Lord Goring, the Earl of Caversham, Sir Robert, Lady and Miss Mabel Chiltern, the Countess of Basildon and Mrs Cheveley; Lady Berkshire is mentioned. Titles in real life commonly adopt place names, so they are quite apt and amusing in drama. The Wildes also visited Bracknell as guests of the mother of Alfred Douglas, Lady Queensberry, who wanted help concerning her son's poor progress at Oxford. In *The Importance of Being Ernest* Wilde used 'Bracknell' as the name of his greatest comic creation. He needed no further inspiration for Lady Bracknell than his own mother, Lady Wilde, but his visit to Lady Queensberry may also have suggested certain traits.

Reading was the unwished-for home of Oscar Wilde from 21 November 1895 to 18 May 1897, during which time his name was C.3.3., the number of his prison cell. The Marquess of Queensberry, angered by his inability to break up the close friendship between his son and Wilde, had insulted the writer both in his house and publicly at his clubs and the theatres where his plays were in production. Caught in the quarrel between father and son, Wilde brought a prosecution for libel against Queensberry, lost his case and was prosecuted in turn by the Crown, because of the evidence brought by his accusers. A string of

OSCAR WILDE

witnesses was found to testify to Wilde's ambiguous sexuality and practices; as a result of the 1885 Criminal Law Amendment Act, which prohibited indecent relations, between consenting adult males, the inevitable verdict resulted.

Wilde was transferred to Reading Gaol after short periods in two London prisons. His physical and mental state was so poor that it was decided to move him to a less severe regime. The prison governor, J Isaacson, flattered to receive so eminent an inmate, arranged for him to work in the garden and the prison library. However, prisoners were forbidden to speak even in the brief periods in the exercise yard, letters and visits were strictly limited and punishment followed every infringement of rules, so life was still onerous. Wilde was almost overcome with misery and remorse many times. On his arrest, his name was removed from posters; plays such as *An Ideal Husband*, which had attracted packed houses to the Haymarket, were taken off, and his books were removed from sale. His debts grew, he was made bankrupt, his house and property were sold. Personal damage to him was vast, as he records in *De Profundis*:

> *my Burne-Jones drawings: my Whistler drawings...my Library with its collection of presentation volumes from almost every poet of my time, from Hugo to Whitman, from Swinburne to Mallarmé, from Morris to Verlaine; with its beautifully bound editions of my father's and my mother's works; its wonderful array of college and school prizes...'*

Reading Gaol above the River Kennet.

Much more was lost, too. Wilde's sadness was to continue: Constance, herself unwell, travelled from Genoa early in 1896 to break the news of his mother's death. Worse was to follow: 'My two children are taken away from me, by legal procedure. That is and will remain to me a source of infinite distress, of distress without end or limit.' Constance and her two sons adopted the name Holland and a guardian was appointed for the boys.

In mid-1896 a new governor, Major JO Nelson, was appointed to Reading Gaol. 'The Home Office has allowed you some books,' he told Wilde, and he also gave him permission to work at some writing. *De Profundis*, a long letter addressed to Alfred Douglas, strongly deplored that young man's mercenary, demanding behaviour and compared his neglect of the author since his trial with the support shown by others. Wilde then explains how his thinking has developed in the long hours in his cell: 'that might bring balm to the bruised heart, and peace to the soul in pain.' He has learned from the prisoners, he says, who did not have a position in life and from the kindness of some of the warders; he speaks much of art but more of religion. He says he should accept his disgrace and punishment; by this means, the healing power of 'the beauty of the sun and moon, the pageant of the seasons, the music of daybreak and the silence of great nights, the rain falling through the leaves, or the dew creeping over the grass and making it silver...' will not be tainted for him. Here he seems to have lost his 'detestation' of nature. Later he argues: 'People point to Reading Gaol, and say "There is where the artistic life leads a man". Well, it might lead one to worse places.'

Wilde was released from prison in May 1897. He spent the rest of his life in France and Italy. He wrote one more poem, *The Ballad of Reading Gaol*. Charles Thomas Wooldridge was hanged in the gaol for the murder of his wife on the road between Windsor and Clewer. This event cast a terrible shadow over everyone in the prison, and it brought much of Wilde's thinking into focus. He writes in simple, strong ballad form:

> *Yet each man kills the thing he loves,*
> *By each let this be heard,*
> *Some do it with a bitter look,*
> *Some with a flattering word.*
> *The coward does it with a kiss,*
> *The brave man with a sword.*

He continues to list the ways that all harm what is the most precious to them, but all do not end in an unmarked grave within prison walls.

Oscar Wilde, poor, ailing and often lonely, died on 30 November 1900 and is buried in Paris. Shortly before that, in a letter to Robert Ross, he had said that he was going on a pilgrimage to the shrine of Notre Dame de Lisse, who his landlady believed 'helps everyone to the spirit of joy'. 'I do not know how long it will take me to get to the shrine, as I must walk. But from what she tells me, it will take at least six or seven minutes to get there and as many to come back. In fact the chapel is just fifty yards from the hotel!'

He enjoyed much longer strolls, too; another friend tells of walking in the French countryside with Wilde at this time: 'We went for a long walk by the River Marne: and I was touched when the exile said, "Might not this be a bit of the Thames?"

OSCAR WILDE – WALK 7

As Oscar Wilde recalled the Thames Valley, so Berkshire remembers him: the Wilde Theatre at South Hill Park, Bracknell, bears his name and the *Reading Chronicle*, in November 1995, celebrated his life and work 'as a great artist'; by 2000, a hundred years after his death, it is hoped that a memorial to him will be placed on Chestnut Walk below Reading Gaol and alongside the Kennet.

WALK 7

AN OSCAR WILDE WALK OF TWO MILES IN CENTRAL READING, WHICH REFERS ALSO TO JANE AUSTEN AND KENNETH GRAHAME

Ordnance Survey Landranger Sheet 175
START POINT: grid reference 717736

OSCAR WILDE SPENT time in various places in Berkshire, as has been outlined, but since it is his unhappy years in Reading Gaol that are likely to be most often remembered, this walk starts in central Reading.

The details of this route apply at the time of writing, but Reading Borough Arts Committee plan to improve the setting of the Abbey Ruins and to put an imposing memorial to Wilde in Chestnut Walk, so minor changes may be necessary once this work has been carried out.

Begin from Reading Town Hall, situated where Blagrave Street joins Market Place. The Town Hall was designed by Alfred Waterhouse, father-in-law of Robert Bridges, and was built 1872–75 in the brickwork for which Reading is noted. Booklets giving fuller details of the history of Reading Abbey and points of interest on the route of this walk are available in the Town Hall's information centre and in the adjoining museum.

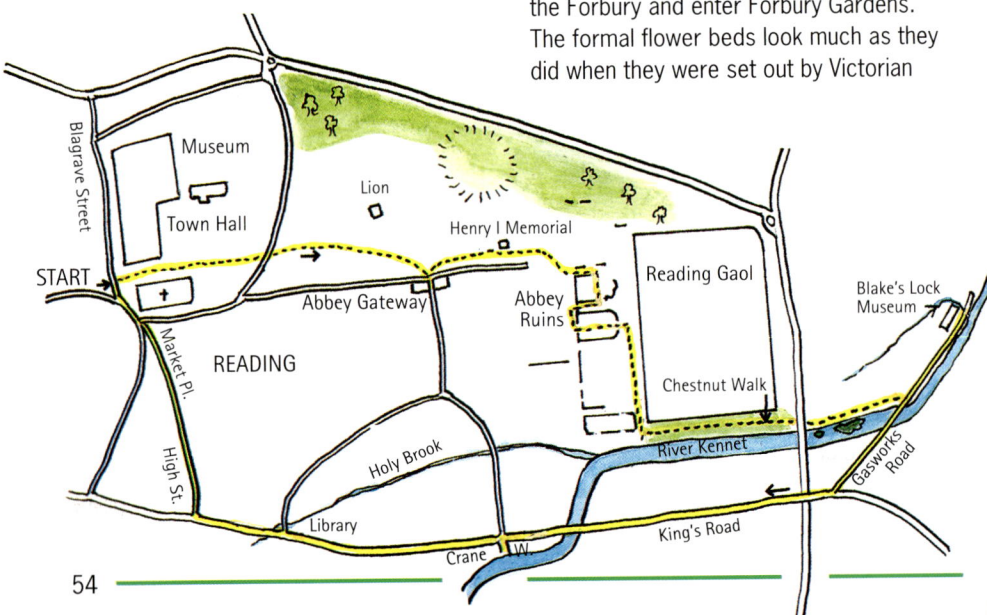

Leave the Square by a passage between No. 1 Friar Street and the very old and beautiful St Lawrence's Church. Beyond the churchyard and the 15th-century Abbey Hospitium on your left, pass through a brick-pillared gateway, carefully cross the the Forbury and enter Forbury Gardens. The formal flower beds look much as they did when they were set out by Victorian gardeners in 1855, and as they did when Wilde was brought to Reading – though it is unlikely that he ever caught a glimpse of their bright colours. Walk on a path diagonally right, passing a stone fountain. The Maiwand Lion, a memorial to men of the Berkshire Regiment killed in the Afghan War, is on your left, as is the bandstand. Turn to the right, to leave the garden by a gate swathed in wisteria.

Across the small road, called Abbot's Walk, is a gateway designed by Gilbert Scott; it was built, in 1861, because the ancient abbey gateway, which had been the home of Mrs La Tournelle's school, attended by Jane Austen and her sister from 1785, had collapsed. WH Fox Talbot photographed the original building in 1845, before it crumbled; his picture looks through the arch of the gateway towards the north, and shows open fields crossed by paths leading to the Thames and woods at Caversham. Look carefully at the new gateway and notice the small steps leading to the room above; these are worn enough to have been part of the earlier structure. A Norman arch also remains within the Victorian re-building. In Jane Austen's schooldays the ruins of the great abbey were surrounded by open space that was used as a site for fairs and other leisure pursuits.

Turn back into Forbury Gardens and then right; on the left is a Memorial Cross to King Henry I, who founded the Abbey in 1121; its main west door stood on this spot. Walk ahead under a tunnel into the Abbey Ruins; little is left, except the flint core of some of the walls but in the first area, formerly the south transept, a plaque on the left marks the burial place of Henry I. Reading, the burial place of a king, can truly be called a Royal Town! Walk to the next space, the Chapter House, where Britain's earliest written four-part harmony, with a verse celebrating the coming of 'Sumer', is engraved. *The Oxford Book of English Verse* has as its first entry 'Sumer is icumen in,' c1250. Beyond are plaques to the first and last bishops of the abbey. Leave by stone steps and turn right down a path on the left of the ruins, with one wall of the gaol, now Reading Remand Centre, on your left.

At the River Kennet, turn left under the chestnut trees and walk ahead, with the wall of the prison again on your left. Woodcuts by Frans Masereel in the 1925 edition of Oscar Wilde's *The Ballad of Reading Gaol* picture the horror of prison life in Wilde's day. A foreword by John Betjeman praises this edition. Walk on, climbing the towpath to a grey iron bridge where, if you look back, you have a good view of the gaol rising from behind its walls. At the road ahead, turn left and find Blake's Lock Museum on the left. This small museum is worth visiting for its records of Reading social history; there is a splendid gypsy caravan that Kenneth Grahame's Mr Toad would have been proud of. Built by Dunton and Sons at Crane Wharf, this is just one example of the coach-building for which Reading was well known. In fact, as well as his caravan, Toad's motor cars, the canal and its barge people, the railway, with its kind engine-driver, and the prison, into which he was thrown, were, in Kenneth Grahame's day, all to be found in the centre of Reading.

To continue the walk, return along Gasworks Road over the bridge, then turn right, to pass the Prudential building, and cross the busy junction into King's Road. The third turning on the left is Crane Wharf, referred to above, where coach-building of caravans and cars took place until the 1930s. Continue along King's Road and find

Reading Main Library on the right; on the fourth floor there is an excellent local studies section, where material used for this book can be studied. Some books can be borrowed.

To complete the route, walk ahead as far as High Street. This leads into Market Place, site of the lending library from which Jane Austen may have borrowed books as a girl, and ahead of you see the Town Hall. In Reading Museum, just beyond the Town Hall, there are a number of fine paintings showing the abbey's inner gateway as it was when Jane Austen knew it.

KENNETH GRAHAME, 1859–1932

KENNETH GRAHAME LIVED a large part of his life by the rivers and on the hills of Berkshire; its woods, meadows, footways and waterways are the setting for much of his writing, in particular the evergreen *Wind in the Willows*. He is less well-known as one who walked the county's countryside often and with energy. His early writing speaks of the pleasure this gives; in *The Romance of the Road*, published in 1891, he claims:

> The best example I know of an approach to this excellent vitality in roads is the Ridgeway of the North Berkshire Downs. Join it at Streatley, the point where it crosses the Thames: at once it strikes you out and away from the habitable world in a splendid purposeful manner, running along the highest ridge of the Downs, a broad green ribbon of turf...such a track is in some sort humanly companionable; it really seems to lead you by the hand.

He speaks of the 'springing stride of the early start' of the walk and the 'pleasant weariness' as the lights of the end 'glimmer through the dusk'; 'after many a mile in sun and wind – maybe rain – you are aching all over and enjoying it' and the 'golden glow of the faculties is only felt at its fulness after prolonged exertion in the open air'. Today's seasoned ramblers do not need such advice; they do owe the preservation of the paths, however, to those who have persuaded their readers to walk for pleasure when travel on foot was no longer a necessity.

Kenneth Grahame first came to live in Berkshire when he was five years old. His mother died of scarlet fever after giving birth to her fourth child. Kenneth too was critically ill with the disease; when he recovered, he woke to a world without his much-loved mother, a loss he felt for the rest of his life. His somewhat feckless father could not cope with four young children, so they left a happy life in Scotland and travelled south to live with their Granny Ingles, at The Mount, Cookham Dene. The eldest child, Helen, later wrote: 'It was hard no doubt, at the age of sixty, having brought up her own family of five sons and a daughter, to have us landed upon her...our grandmother's income was a small one and if our uncle had not helped us I don't know what would have become of us.'

The Mount, a beautiful and rambling house with a three-hundred-year-old oak tree in the grounds, which marked the former edge of Windsor Forest, is set in several acres of gardens and orchard. Near by lies Quarry Wood, and meadows sweep down to the Thames. The Grahame children roamed with freedom through wild orchard and roomy attic; Kenneth's memory of this period of his life was so vivid that when he brought his family back to live in Cookham in 1907 he wrote: 'I feel I should never be surprised to meet myself, as I was when a little chap of five, suddenly coming round a corner...I can remember everything I felt then....'

The Mount was their home for only two years; in 1865, in a heavy gale, a chimney fell and it became clear the house needed much repair. By spring, Granny Inglis and the young Grahames had moved to a much smaller house, ten miles away in Cranbourne. They were to live in Fernhill Cottage, near to Windsor Great Park, for an even shorter time. Their father suddenly took his children home to Inveraray. Kenneth had high hopes, voiced by his Prince in *The Romance of the Rail*, written in 1891: 'I will look upon my father's face again, though the leagues be long to my own land.' Travel to where 'the bright sun shone upon leaping streams and purple heather' was a good memory, but he continues 'Return, indeed, was bitter'.

For a year, they saw how heavy drinking had changed their father, then in 1867 he resigned from his post and went abroad. The children moved south again.

Kenneth Grahame's yearning for his lost family and its re-creation in the mind of the child is reflected in much of what he wrote during the rest of his life. *The Golden Age* and *Dream Days*, essays about childhood, and *The Wind in the Willows*, with its more than a hundred editions, alike recreate a world for those who have not lost the wonder of early youth.

School days at St Edwards, Oxford, were not always happy ones. Grahame says of his first months there, he was a 'small school-boy kicked out of his nest into the draughty, uncomfortable outer world'. He had always found learning to be easy; sister Helen writes with some scorn that he first began to 'spout poetry' at Cranbourne: 'first Shakespeare, then Macaulay Lays then Tennyson...on walks through the pinewoods.' At St Edwards he made very sound progress, winning classics prizes and in his last year becoming Head of School. He wrote essays for, and edited, the school *Chronicle* and enjoyed exploring medieval Oxford and the country that in the 1880s still lay just beyond the city's bridges. We can infer from some of his later writing that he paddled a canoe on the Thames, looking at Oxfordshire bridges, locks and river life:

> *The two influences which most soaked into me there, and have remained with me ever since, were the good grey Gothic, and the cool secluded reaches of the Thames – the 'Stripling Thames', remote and dragon-fly haunted, before it attains to the noise and flannels of Folly Bridge.*

In Kenneth's last year at school the family had to endure yet another loss; his youngest brother, Willie, died of lung trouble on New Year's Eve 1895; he was just sixteen.

After school Kenneth Grahame hoped to go to Oxford University and follow an academic career. However, his Uncle John felt the cost of four years at Oxford could not be justified, despite Grahame's protests. So a vacancy was found in his uncle's office and, three years later, a clerkship in the Bank of England. To the young man this was a serious blow, which he felt would affect him for the rest of his life.

Holidays offered compensations; often these were spent away from London in quiet but vigorous activity. Sidney Ward, a colleague from the Bank, recalled a weekend he spent with Grahame

> ...at Streatley, during a cold, sunny spring. A friend had lent him a fourteenth-century cottage in the main street and we had a grand twenty-mile walk along the Ridgeway...we came home happy and tired, bought some chops and fetched a huge jug of beer from the pub. We cooked our dinner over the open wood fire...how good the chops were! Then great chunks of cheese, new bread, great swills of beer, pipes, bed and heavenly sleep.

To become a published writer was a natural way for a young man to make his mark if an academic career was denied him. Kenneth Grahame had been born in Castle Street, Edinburgh, near where Walter Scott had lived for twenty-four years. Grahame's father had loved reciting chosen parts of Scott's novels and was a fair, if secret, poet; literary pursuits were a natural part of home life. Robert Louis Stevenson, nine years older than Grahame and also Scottish, was writing as an essayist and his success inspired the younger man.

Literary life in London played its part, too. Dining on his own in Soho, he noticed a lively group, with a lion-like man at its centre; he was asked to join them and found he had met FJ Furnivall, who was then editing the *New English Dictionary* and founding literary societies. Dr Furnivall persuaded Grahame to become Honorary Secretary of the New Shakespeare Society, and as a result he met Browning, Swinburne and other leading writers. Furnivall was also a practising and dedicated Socialist, who would lead slum children round Kew Gardens. Such pursuits appealed to Grahame's dislike of privilege and his love of the open air. At this time, also, he found that Pantheism, with its belief that all natural life is God, had values that rang true for him.

The Bank of England at that time was a livelier place to work in than Grahame had thought it would be, and his career there progressed. He was content to write for fun and publish when he could. Dr Furnivall, when he was shown essays and poems, advised that the prose was most promising. One of the first essays to bear his name appeared in the *St James' Gazette* in 1888. *By a Northern Furrow* speaks of the Berkshire Downs in winter. He tells how the downs had seen 'Saxon levies' confront the 'Danish invader' and describes how the furrows in the valley gleam red on the side they turn to the winter sun although on the 'breezy top of the Downs' the turf is 'still virgin'. Although somewhat laboured, this writing shows a careful observation of natural detail; the subject matter, of real interest to the writer, is fresh to the reader. Other essays on landscape or wildlife themes were published. *A Woodland at Home* in 1890 and *The Rural Pan* in 1891, both appeared in the *National Observer*. By 1893 Grahame had published his first volume of collected essays, titled *Pagan Papers*. *The Golden Age* followed in 1895 and *Dream Days* in 1898; these descriptions were based on memories of his Berkshire childhood; it was in them that he found his true voice. The stories, narrated by the boy, describe childhood's private world. Clearly based on the Grahame children and their cousins, they give insight into any child's imagination and a child's view of the baffling adult world; they delighted both critics and public alike. In the first essay of *The Golden Age*, the Olympians, or adults, 'spent much of their time stuffily indoors'.

For them the orchard (a place elf-haunted, wonderful!) simply produced so many apples and cherries: or it didn't, when the failures of Nature were not infrequently ascribed to us. They never set foot in fir wood or hazel copse, nor dreampt of the marvels hid therein. The mysterious sources, sources as of old Nile, that fed the duckpond had no magic for them...They cared not about exploring for robbers' caves, nor digging for hidden treasure.

In July 1899, when he was forty and she was thirty-seven, Grahame married Elspeth Thompson. They had both been born in Edinburgh and now lived in London, both had lost parents early, and both were used to meeting famous people. Elspeth, as hostess for her wealthy stepfather, had met many leading figures in the fields of literature, science and art. After much hesitation, Kenneth and Elspeth married in Fowey, in Cornwall, where Grahame had spent many holidays with close friends. Although she had grand wedding clothes with her, the bride chose to wear white muslin and a daisy chain. A son, Alistair, was born within a year, but the marriage was disappointing to both partners. Kenneth was too long set in bachelor ways to change, and Elspeth was left alone, writing sad little verses, and unable to share his imaginative depth. Soon she wrote:

I cannot keep your love
I may not give you mine
Take up your flowers and glove
Let others see no sign.

Alistair, nicknamed Mouse, grew up with the handicap of being more than half blind. In spite of this, his parents, especially Elspeth, regarded him as a prodigy; his father began telling him stories of Mole, Badger and Water Rat while he was still in his pram, and was delighted when the child corrected his memory of the details.

Grahame did not want Mouse to grow up an urban child; in 1906 he leased a house, The Hillyers, near his old haunts in Cookham Dene. Mouse, now six years old, was delighted and more so when his father found a larger house, Mayfield, which 'low and rambling, thatched and meadow-bordered, was an idyll of elms and buttercups and old red brick'. With

Mouse and friends, Grahame explored the countryside and one summer day, a visitor recalled how he tried to summon a creature in Quarry Wood using 'a most alluring whistle'. Grahame said 'There's a Water Rat down there, at least it's his home; he's quite a friend of mine. Evidently he's gone on some excursion – I shall hear about it one day.' In *The Rural Pan*, the god, like the writer, sought out the quiet places: 'In the hushed recesses of Hurley backwater, where the canoe may be paddled almost under the tumbling comb of the weir, he is to be looked for; there the god pipes with the freest abandonment.'

Mouse so loved his bedtime stories – especially now Mr Toad had made his appearance in them – that he refused to go on holiday to Littlehampton, while his parents visited friends in Fowey, until his father promised to send further instalments by post. These letters were the basis of Grahame's classic, *The Wind in the Willows*. He had written little for nine years and took some persuading, but once committed, he worked with energy. From Mouse's memories, from the much-studied countryside and the wild creatures of the Thames, from the woods and downs of Berkshire, from the boating at Fowey and from the thinking and prose developed over many years, Kenneth Grahame distilled a tale that is a perpetual delight.

Two contemporary letters show how far the little book travelled; President Theodore Roosevelt, writing from the White House in Washington, USA, in 1909, said 'at first he could not reconcile to animals after the first books' but when his wife and sons 'Kermit and Ted, all quite independently took such delight in it' he took note. As Mrs Roosevelt read it aloud for the younger children, he listened: 'Now I have read it and reread it and have come to accept the characters as old friends...indeed I feel about going to Africa very much as the sea-faring rat did, when he almost made the water-rat wish to forsake every thing and start wandering.' The Hon. Alfred Deakin, then Prime Minister of Australia, explained that he had enjoyed the earlier books but found *The Wind in the Willows* 'a prose poem perfect within its scope, style and sentiment and rising to a climax in the vision of Pan – a piece of imaginative insight, to which it would be hard to find a parallel anywhere.'

Grahame had been promoted to Secretary of the Bank in 1898, but a severe chest infection a year later and a long journey to work from Cookham had reduced his interest and efficiency and he resigned in 1908, four months before the publication of *The Wind in the Willows*. In spite of his love of the Thames Valley and his acceptance that it was the natural home of his small animal friends, he became tired of the influx of incomers with their toad-like talk of motor cars and steam launches. In 1910 he moved house again with his family; Grahame's rhyme gives their new address:

At Boham's, Blewbury, Didcot, Berks.
She would wake in the morning and listen to larks.

Boham's was a little old farmhouse where there was not much space 'in a very beautiful village, with the Downs at one's door,' as Grahame wrote to a friend. 'I hope for some very fine walking, when I have finished picture-hanging and falling over rolls of carpet.' In another letter he describes going to the big annual sheep fair at East Ilsley and finding it lively: 'The noise of dogs and sheep, the droves of flock masters and dealers in the most fascinating clothes you can conceive...the beautiful little village all glittering with movement and humming with the real Berkshire language'; when he found Mouse 'bidding at the auction for the pedigree rams' he had 'to haul him out of there'.

Life was not all happy, however. Mouse's education brought many problems: Elspeth's inflated view of her son's ability, the child's very poor eyesight, his precocious manner and speech made him a natural target for bullies. He was sent to Rugby School, where he lasted for two weeks, then at Eton unhappiness again resulted in his leaving after two terms. A tutor was found and progress was better; swimming and horse-riding even gave much enjoyment. In 1918 Alistair, by his father's influence, gained entry to Christ Church, Oxford, and trouble began again; he failed some exams and struggled through others. That other problems affected him during those years is very likely. He left College one evening, walked across fields and was run over by a train. Doubts were expressed at the inquest over whether death had been accidental; his parents clung firmly to a belief that it had been. He was buried in Holywell cemetery, and his headstone reads:

Here was laid to rest on his twentieth birthday, 12th of May 1920, Alistair, only child of Kenneth and Elspeth Grahame, of whose noble ideals, steadfast purposes and rare promise remains only a loved and honoured memory.

By October that year the Grahames' most valuable property had been sold, Boham's farmhouse had been let and the couple set out for Italy. They stayed in Rome but visited many other cities and localities. On holiday in the Dolomites, Grahame still walked; he was seen 'striding over hill and dale, his Inverness cape swirling around him, his hair all swept up by the wind. On and on he went, solitary, absorbed in his own thoughts, until he vanished in the distance.'

In 1924 they returned to England; they sold Boham's and bought Church Cottage, Pangbourne. Although they now lived in the centre of this fashionable riverside resort, their own lives changed little. Elderly and even eccentric, especially Elspeth, who wore clothes from jumble sales and was mean in her dealings with tradesmen, they found pleasure in the quiet of the garden. Grahame loved 'the sweep of the lawn bordered by a bank of oriental poppies, the fruit trees and the sunny terrace', where he would sit to read the paper. The Thames was just a three-minute stroll away and travel to sunnier climes was a feature of many winters.

Kenneth Grahame did little literary work after *The Wind in the Willows*. Because of his love of the circus, he wrote a foreword for *Seventy Years a Showman*, the memoirs of George Sanger and he produced some papers and poems for special events, but he firmly refused to begin an autobiography. A new edition of *The Wind in the Willows*, illustrated by EH Shepard, was published in 1930; in the same year AA Milne's *Toad of Toad Hall* was staged and became a classic in its own right. Inevitably it puts the story into pantomime form and Milne admitted that he could not transplant the lyrical style of the original. Other stage versions have followed.

KENNETH GRAHAME

Church Cottage, Pangbourne and St James the Less Church.

Kenneth Grahame died in 1932. At his funeral in St James the Less, the church was filled with flowers and cards from children countrywide. He was buried later, next to his son in Holywell, near Oxford. Walkers can remember him by words from *The Felowe that Goes Alone*. In this he says 'Nature's particular gifts to the walker, the sun and the wind, the road and the dusty hedges' are 'to set the mind free to think'; he adds that the road 'should always give way to the field path when choice offers'.

Berkshire gave Kenneth Grahame much of the material for his writing – the river for the homes of his small animals; the great houses alongside it for Toad Hall, the woods for the wild-wooders, the gaol, the canal and railway for Toad's adventures – and so he always saw himself returning to live in some 'sequestered reach of the quiet Thames'. In return, he created for his readers a unique world for them to recall as they stride across its high downs, row quietly along its backwaters or wander in its valleys.

As two Berkshire villages, along with the country surrounding them, form the main settings for the life and work of Kenneth Grahame, two walks are given.

THE FIRST WALK starts at the war memorial, on the Green in Cookham Dean. Cookham Dean is four miles north-west of Maidenhead.

KENNETH GRAHAME – WALK 8

WALK 8

A KENNETH GRAHAME WALK OF THREE AND A HALF MILES FROM COOKHAM DEAN

Ordnance Survey Landranger Sheet 175
START POINT: grid reference 872853

FROM THE MEMORIAL, walk south-west up Church Road, passing the Church of St John the Baptist on your left. Fork left into Spring Lane, taking care because there are few verges to walk on in this part of the lane; there are plenty of fine gardens to see, however, in spring or any season. After about half a mile the lane descends, passing on the left the wooded grounds of The Mount, where the Grahame children came to live with their Granny Inglis in 1864. At a post box go left into a minor lane and pass Mount Lodge. The Mount itself is away in the trees but the other houses give some idea of the extent of the estate in 1864, when its grounds extended to the Thames. At the junction, turn right and after a few yards pass the gateway to Mount Farm on your left.

Continue ahead on Choke Lane for about 500 yards, then turn right on to a bridleway through trees, leading into a field. Walk ahead to the field corner, then turn right, keeping the hedge on your left, to reach a National Trust car park. From this, cross Winter Hill Road, and then a plank bridge into a field. Turn right along a path through an open field, then enter Bisham Woods. This name applies to a whole range of woods on the ridge overlooking the Thames; the part you have reached is Quarry Wood, known well by Grahame both as a boy and as a grown-up, when he brought his son back to Cookham Dean.

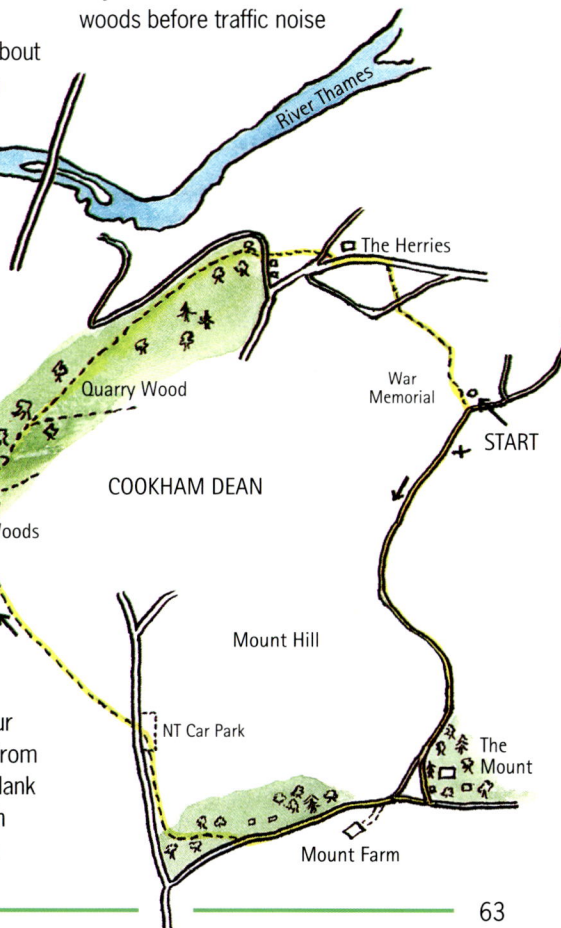

Walk ahead and, at path signs, continue downhill in the same direction; at a wide track, continue ahead on the path opposite. When this ends at a junction turn up right and on reaching a fork, take the left, marked footpath. Keep ahead, passing wide views on the left of Marlow, with the Thames winding below and the Chiltern Hills gently rising beyond. Grahame knew these woods before traffic noise ruined their peace! Keep ahead, with the motorway noise receding, and when the path reaches a wood of large trees follow it round right to reach a road. Cross this road, enter a footpath to the left of the end house in the row opposite and go ahead, ignoring cross-paths, to reach the road. Cross a small green ahead and turn left along Dean Lane to come to the house called The Hillyers, which the Grahame family rented in 1906. The Herries Preparatory School occupied the property until recently. A plaque records that 'Kenneth Grahame, 1859–1932, Author, lived here'.

Continue down the hill and turn right on a footpath opposite Job's Lane. Cross the road at the end, climb a grassy path ahead and turn left on to a gravel track that leads up back to the Green and the war memorial.

'Mayfield', another house where Grahame lived, no longer exists.

THE SECOND WALK begins from the public car park in Station Road, Pangbourne, and looks at Kenneth Grahame's last home and its neighbourhood.

WALK 9

A KENNETH GRAHAME WALK OF FIVE MILES FROM PANGBOURNE, WHICH ALSO PASSES PLACES LINKED WITH LYTTON STRACHEY, DH LAWRENCE AND JEROME K JEROME

Ordnance Survey Landranger Sheet 175
START POINT: grid reference 634765

BEGIN BY TAKING a path running alongside the car park and leading past a Scout hut and into the churchyard of the Church of St James the Less, which the Grahames attended. The first house beyond the churchyard and up the road to the right is Church Cottage. Behind its high fence, it looks much as it did in the 1920s. The small round building in the corner of the garden was the village lock-up in years gone by.

To resume the walk, turn left past the church then right into High Street, which crosses the River Pang as it flows through some pleasant gardens. Keep on the right side of the street, then turn right into Reading Road. Walk ahead, noticing such shops as Ducks' Ditty, to reach a public footpath on the right and a house called Wild Wood, perhaps named by another admirer of

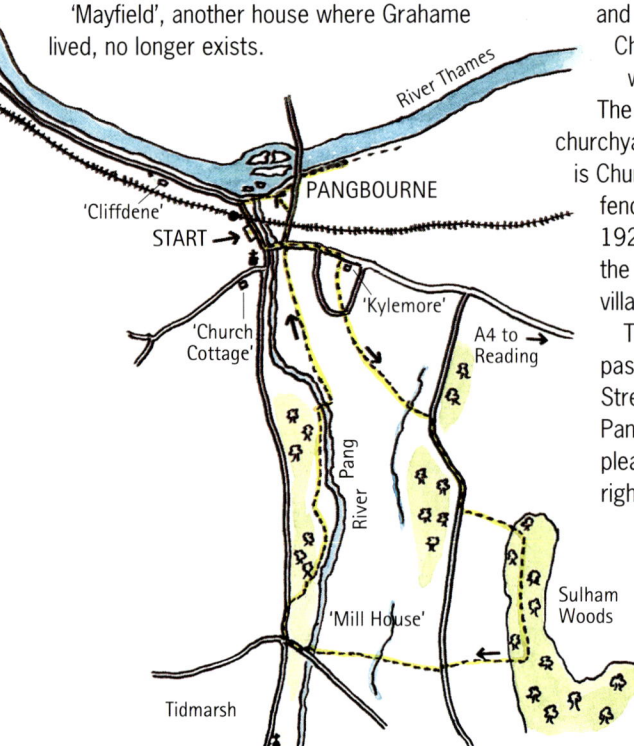

The Wind in the Willows. The house to the left of the path, Kylemore, was called The Myrtles when it was home to DH Lawrence for short periods in 1919. Now take the footpath and continue ahead, as it crosses a road and passes left of allotments.

Take the gate into a field and follow the path ahead across small bridges and a stile to reach Sulham Lane. Walk right and after a left bend, leave the lane by a footpath on the left. Climb a clear path to reach a gate into Sulham Woods, then go up steps and turn right into a wide permitted path under beech trees; birdsong can be heard and Grahame's small mammals can be imagined in their 'wild wood'. Turn right over a stile when you reach a path that crosses and walk down to the bottom of the field. Turn right for a short distance then left over a stile to reach the road again.

Walk a few steps left to a path on the right over a small bridge and, by trees, white posts and ahead to pillboxes. Cross a backwater and stile to pass more pillboxes now on your left. After a stile, reach a bridge over the River Pang. Water Rat, Mole, and their picnic, can be imagined floating quietly along such small rivers. Mr Toad is more at home on the wide Thames with its grand houses.

Leaving the Pang, reach Sulham Road; opposite is Mill House, home of Lytton Strachey from 1917 to 1924. Here, in the privacy afforded by its large garden and orchard (in which a Roman bath was fed from a mill stream), he corrected proofs of *Eminent Victorians* and began work on his biography of Queen Victoria.

Turn right, passing Mill House and its mill stones, and turn right into the main road. A short way after the Greyhound, go right from the main road through a gate on to an enclosed path that leads past gardens to a drive. Turn left for a few steps, then take stiles on the right to cross small paddocks and reach a path alongside the Pang. Where this ends, turn right over a footbridge and stile and walk along by the bank until the river bends left. Here keep ahead to a swing gate and follow a fenced path and small road to reach Reading Road. Cross into Whitchurch Road, which leads towards the Thames. Before the river, walk right through a car park and into Pangbourne Meadows, where Grahame often strolled.

To continue, leave the meadows and return a short way along Whitchurch Road and soon take a footpath on the right, which gives good views of weirs and the lock; there is a small public grassy patch with seats. Grahame also came this way when EH Shepherd prepared illustrations for the 1931 edition of T*he Wind in the Willows*.

Continue the walk by following this path into Station Road. By turning right into Shooter's Hill, you reach the much-painted Swan Inn, named by Jerome 'quaint' and 'little'; today, if it is fine, a more apt word might be 'busy'. Continue along Shooter's Hill to an imposing Victorian house on the left called Cliffdene; here, it is claimed, DH Lawrence stayed as a guest when he had to move away from the cottage in Hermitage. This house is the first of seven in a row, called The Seven Deadly Sins. To return to the start point, walk back along Shooter's Hill and under a bridge in Station Road. Before you go into the car park, pause at the village sign, which commemorates its favourite author.

The Grahame family home from 1910 to 1920 was in Blewbury. Take the A417 from Reading; Boham's Farmhouse, now called

Boham's House, is in Westbrook Street, Blewbury. The road is on the right, near the end of the village, and the house is on the right-hand side of Westbrook Street, rather hemmed in by Grahame Close, recently built and named after the writer, of course. It is likely the Grahames took the footpath from the main road on the opposite side to Westbrook Street to reach Churn Hill, the Ridgeway and the downs.

JEROME KLAPKA JEROME, 1859–1927

JEROME KLAPKA JEROME'S famous *Three Men in a Boat* might give the impression that he and his friends were typical of the modern young men who Kenneth Grahame felt were spoiling the peace of the Thames countryside. The trio, 'to say nothing of the dog', met up where the Wey, the Bourne and the Basingstoke Canal 'all enter the Thames together'. On reaching this point the first thing they saw

...was George's blazer on one side of the lock gates, closer inspection showing that George was inside it. Montmorency set up a furious barking, I shrieked, Harris roared; George waved his hat and yelled back. The lock-keeper rushed out with a drag, under the impression that someone had fallen into the lock, and appeared annoyed at finding that no one had. George had rather a curious oilskin-covered parcel in his hand. It was round and flat at one end...a long straight handle sticking out of it.
'What's that?' said Harris, 'a frying-pan?'
'No,' said George, with a strange, wild look glittering in his eyes, 'they are all the rage this season; everybody has got them up the river. It's a banjo.'
'I never knew you played the banjo!' Harris and I said together.
'Not exactly,' replied George; 'but it's very easy, they tell me; and I've got the instruction book!'

Such foolery gives a misleading image of Jerome, however. He and Grahame were born in the same year and their lives traced similar paths, in many respects. Jerome's father was of middle-class puritan stock and trained for a Nonconformist ministry. He was never ordained, but he became a fluent preacher and was known as Reverend Jerome. His mother, daughter of a solicitor, brought some wealth to their marriage. After attempts to farm in Devon and mine for silver, they moved to Walsall, where the coal business was booming. Much money was invested, but their pits only did well after the Jeromes, by now quite poor, were forced to abandon the venture and move to genteel poverty in London's East End.

The fourth child, Jerome, had been born in Walsall; his middle name was changed from Clapp to Klapka after the Hungarian General, who stayed with the family while he wrote his memoirs. Family sadness affected Jerome's early life; his elder brother, Milton, died when just six years old, and when his father died Jerome was only twelve and he fairly soon became the main breadwinner. In spite of this, he reports in his autobiography, *My Life and Times*, that he felt his family were 'rather fortunate folk' as they 'lived in the biggest house in Suffolk Street', furnished beautifully 'with china and fine pictures', a 'semi-grand piano', and damask curtains; there was a garden where his mother watered the 'mignonette and nasturtiums'. Jerome was taught at home until he was ten years old, then he won a place at the Philological School in Lisson Grove, a long journey from home. This meant rising very early, but he enjoyed exploring and his season ticket allowed him to wander. Later, in *Paul Kelver*, a novel based closely on his early years, he wrote of an encounter with an elderly gentleman in Victoria Park, Hackney. He was fairly sure he had met Charles Dickens: 'and told him "I am going to be an author when I grow up, and write books." He took my hand in his and shook it gravely, then returned it to me.'

After asking about the boy's favourite reading, which included 'Scott, Dumas, Hugo, Marlowe and de Quincy', the gentleman continued:

> *'And what do you think of Mr Dickens?' he asked. But he did not seem very interested in the subject. He had picked up a few small stones and was throwing them carefully into the water.*
> *'I like him very much,' I answered;*
> *'he makes you laugh.'*
> *'Not always?' he asked. He had stopped his stone-throwing and turned sharply towards me.*
> *'Oh, no, not always,' I admitted; 'but I like the funny bits best.'*

At fourteen, Jerome began work as a railway clerk at Euston Station and his twenty-six pounds a year, eked out by a little extra from overtime, supported his sister until she married and his mother until she died in 1873. Still only fifteen, lonely and confused, he found lodgings in a succession of Camden Town rooms; typically, when space had been made for the bed, a washstand, 'straw-coloured, with staring white basin and jug', a couple of chairs, 'which did not pretend to be easy', and a home-made table, three square feet was left for the tenant. Just such a room would feature later in his career in the title of his best-known play, *The Passing of the Third Floor Back*. In *My Life and Times* he writes: 'I had friends and relatives in London, who I am sure would have been kind, but my poverty increased my shyness; I had a dread of asking.'

Jerome did not forget his wish to become a writer, but at first he found it easier to make friends and to increase his earnings through part-time acting. Modest success tempted him to join theatrical touring companies. However, after three years, disillusioned, he returned to London, poorer than before. His experience of Victorian touring groups, however, gave him material for a series of amusing essays that appeared in *The Play*; in 1885 these were adapted for his first published book, *On the Stage – and Off*. Jerome, although by day a solicitor's clerk, was encouraged by the success of his first book and decided to write more essays, using the same gently humorous style. *The Idle Thoughts of an Idle Fellow*, published in 1886, again sold well. He also wrote a number of plays at this time.

Jerome's marriage in 1888 to Georgina Stanley proved to be a happy one. He later wrote of time spent by the Thames, which by then he knew well.

> Most of my life I have dwelt in the neighbourhood of the river. I thank Old Father Thames for many happy

days. We spent our honeymoon, my wife and I, in a little boat. I knew the river well, its deep pools, and hidden ways, its quiet backwaters, its sleepy towns and villages.

It is not surprising, then, that a Thames journey was the subject of his next book. The three river adventurers knew each other well. Jerome and bank clerk George Wingrave had shared a room from early in the 1880s, and Carl Hentschel, the Harris of the book, was another close friend. The three formed the core of several clubs of young 'vagabonds' and theatre-goers; they encouraged each other and had made river trips on more than one occasion. In *My Life and Times* Jerome explains that his book was to be *The Story of the Thames, its scenery and history*, with 'humorous relief'. Just back from honeymoon, he wrote the amusing anecdotes first, and quickly finished them. A dozen 'slabs of history' were then added, one in each chapter. FW Robinson, however, who was publishing the sections in serial form in *Home Chimes*, rejected most of the serious material and asked for a new title. Jerome chose *Three Men in a Boat* 'because nothing else seemed right'. The descriptive and historical passages that remained link the humorous episodes and mark the progress of the friends upriver.

Most ramblers are interested in knowing more about the routes they walk; is the sign described here, for instance, still near the Thames towpath?:

The 'George and Dragon' at Wargrave boasts a sign, painted on the one side by Leslie RA, and on the other by Hodgson of that ilk. Leslie has depicted the fight; Hodgson has shown the scene after the 'Fight' – George, the work done, enjoying his pint of beer.

Is Sonning still as described by Jerome?

...the most fairy-like little nook on the whole river. It is more like a stage village than one built of bricks and mortar. Every house is smothered in roses, and now, in early June, they were bursting forth in clouds of dainty splendour.

Has The Bull in Sonning still 'low, quaint rooms and latticed windows, and awkward stairs and winding passages'? No doubt 'village politics' is still a frequent topic of gossip with those who sit in the courtyard in front. Perhaps the Thames, near Reading, has improved since the three friends passed by: 'The river is dirty and dismal here. One does not linger in the neighbourhood of Reading,' writes Jerome. But he does say that the town has a notable history: 'Henry I lies buried at Reading, in the Benedictine abbey founded by him there, the ruins of which may still be seen; and, in this same abbey, great John of Gaunt was married to the Lady Blanche.'

The comedy in *Three Men in a Boat* comes from the writer's ability to make a good story out of a very trivial incident. There is the sheer absurdity of the antics of the three friends as they try to open a can of pineapple with a pocket knife, scissors, a

Carl Hentschel (Harris)
George Wingrave (George)
Jerome K. Jerome ('J')

hitcher and a sharp stone because the tin-opener had been left behind; the tin, which by then had been 'battered into every shape known to geometry', was finally flung 'far into the middle of the river' as the three hurled their curses at it. Exaggeration, also intrinsic to most humour, embellishes incidents. The party, accompanied by Montmorency, the dog, went 'marketing after breakfast'; their provisions were carried back to the boat by seventeen assorted people with a variety of baskets and hampers escorted by eight dogs. The boatman's question, when they reach the landing stage, adds to the sense of fun: 'Let me see, sir; was yours a steam-launch or a house-boat?' When told that 'it was a double-sculling skiff, he seemed surprised'.

Jerome wrote that Montmorency, who turned a sceptical eye on much that was involved in the river trip, was an imaginary creation; the only pet he had owned by that time was 'a water rat'. He owned dogs later; one, called Max, accompanied him on long walks, during which new themes and characters were developed.

One anecdote flows neatly into another: 'We had a good deal of trouble with steam-launches that morning,' he continues – a considerable understatement in terms of what followed! Many stories end with a surprising twist; George and Jerome 'went for a walk to Wallingford' and, calling in at a riverside inn, noticed a monstrous trout, displayed in a 'dusty old glass case'. Four local anglers, one being the landlord, in turn gave graphic and varying details of how they each had caught the fish. This is amusing enough, but it is all capped by the final sentences of the chapter: George

The Bull Inn, Sonning.

climbs up to get a better look, the chair slips, he and the case crash to the ground and the trout ends up in a thousand pieces.

> We thought it strange and unaccountable that a stuffed trout should break up into little pieces like that.
> And so it would have been strange and unaccountable, if it had been a stuffed trout, but it was not.
> That trout was plaster of Paris.

Such small extracts cannot do justice to any book. Running all through *Three Men in a Boat* is the River Thames and all the pleasures it holds on or beside its waters, along with details of its scenery and its history. There is the fun, and the mishaps, of the three heroes, which we share – things like this have, or nearly have, happened to us. From the day of its publication in 1889, the public loved it, and copies sold fast. A few early critics disliked the 'vulgarity' of the language, but it is partly because of this fresh and lively style that the book has become a classic. In translation it has sold widely across the world, it has appeared in at least three film versions and it has been adapted for television.

With his literary popularity now assured, Jerome wrote more essays like *The Second Thoughts of an Idle Fellow* and fresh travels by the three adventurers, *Three Men on The Bummel*, which described a cycle trip in Germany. *Paul Kelver*, published in 1902, is a novel, more serious in tone, which traces the early life of a young man very much like Jerome himself. He wrote many plays, some from a social stance shared by later dramatists; most influential was the morality play *The Passing of the Third Floor Back*. He also edited two magazines from 1892, until a libel action in 1897 forced him to sell his interest in them. Work by Rudyard Kipling, Conan Doyle, Robert Louis Stevenson and Oscar Wilde appeared in *The Idler* and in *Today*.

The Jerome family first lived in Berkshire in 1902, when they bought 'Goulds Grove', near Wallingford, which at that time was in Berkshire. In *My Life and Times* Jerome describes it as 'a lonely spot in the Chilterns'. He wrote in a summerhouse in the garden called The Nook. Some idea of the Jeromes' life in the country can be gleaned from *They and I*, a light-hearted novel, published in 1909, which deals with the way the parents and children of a family cope with each other and the demands of their new surroundings. The father is a humorist in his mid-fifties and there are three children in the book: Robina and Dick, who are nearly grown up, and Veronica, the youngest, who appears to be about ten. The Jeromes' daughter, Rowena, an only child, could have been the model for untidy, energetic Veronica, but the others were added for the structure of the book.

In the novel the family wanted a house facing south-west on a hill with an uninterrupted view, on sandy soil, but near the river. Of course their house in fact has few of these features. When Dick finds out it is two miles from the river by road, he asks 'And by the shortest way?'. He is told 'there's a prettier way through the woods but that is about three miles and a half'. Having yearned for the peace of the country, the family find they are woken by birds at dawn and a cow that needs to be milked. When 'a yokel' is

WALK 10

A JEROME K JEROME WALK OF FOUR MILES FROM SONNING, WHICH REFERS ALSO TO JANE AUSTEN

Ordnance Survey Landranger Sheet 175
START POINT: grid reference 756756

---

found to look after the animals, he does not add a rustic tone; he is a Cockney from 'Camden Tahn'. He is promised half a sovereign if he can learn 'Berkshire' and is told 'When you informed me that the cow was mine, you should have said "Whoi, 'er be your cow, surelie 'er be"'. Hopkins, the lad, asks 'Sure it's Berkshire?' and learns 'It may not be Berkshire pure and undefiled; in literature we term it "dialect"'. Much of this is the humorist at work, but there are hints that Jerome was aware that work in the country can be hard: one day Dick is very tired; he is learning farm work and has had to herd three hundred sheep all the way from Ilsley – the same sheep fair, perhaps, as that attended by Kenneth Grahame.

There is little in Jerome's comic writing about walking, but in *My Life and Times* there are references to using footpaths and crossing stiles. When HG Wells was staying with him at Goulds Grove, they 'climbed a lonely spur of the Chilterns', reached the top and gazed 'down upon the towers of Oxford and the Cotswold Hills beyond. At their feet they saw '...now rutted and grass-grown – the long straight line of the old Roman way that led from Grimm's Dyke, past the camp on the Sinodun Hills, and so onward to the north'.

Jerome K Jerome died in 1927, while on a family holiday in Devon. He is buried with other family members in the beautiful churchyard in Ewelme, across the Thames from Wallingford. His writing gives a unique view of Berkshire's beauty; we travel through the county on its main river, with three men and a dog in a small boat; we also climb with him on to its highest hills.

THIS WALK BEGINS in Sonning, which Jerome described as 'the most fairy-like nook on the whole river'. It follows the Thames along to Reading's outskirts and proves that the riverbank is no longer 'dirty and dismal' and is now well worth lingering by.

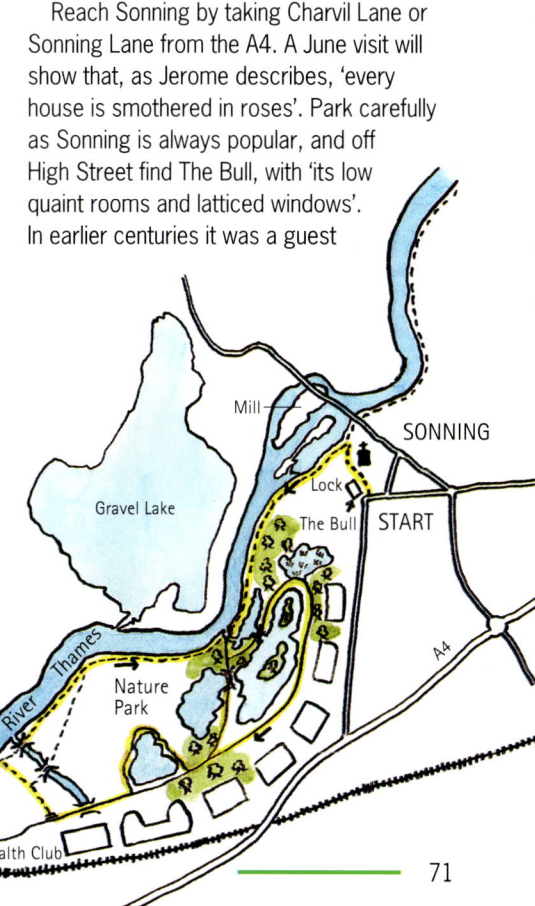

Reach Sonning by taking Charvil Lane or Sonning Lane from the A4. A June visit will show that, as Jerome describes, 'every house is smothered in roses'. Park carefully as Sonning is always popular, and off High Street find The Bull, with 'its low quaint rooms and latticed windows'. In earlier centuries it was a guest house for pilgrims. Walk past the inn and enter the churchyard by its Victorian gate. There was a Saxon church on this site and some traces of twelfth-century building remain in Saint Andrew's, but most of what can be seen today dates from 1852. In 1784 Jane Austen's uncle, Reverend Edward Cooper, was made rector; she may have visited, though no records of this have been traced.

Walk left of the church porch and, at the corner of the churchyard, turn right and follow a path down to the Thames. Turn left along the towpath to Sonning Lock, where the lock gardens are a splendid sight in summer. A map put up by the Environment Agency is worth study, as is a poem singing Sonning's praises.

The river widens as you continue along the towpath, with water meadows in some places and, through the trees, glimpses of lakes. These have been formed from gravel pits and attract much wildlife. After walking about half a mile from Sonning Lock, turn left on to a path away from the river and into a nature reserve. Business development has created this area in the low-lying land near the river and, after quite a short time, water plants, coots, ducks and rarer birds are flourishing.

At the first path junction, there is a choice to be made. Either turn left to walk round the larger pond or turn right for a shorter walk. Both routes join before you go over a stone bridge near a health club. Beyond the bridge, turn right through a gate into a field; public access to the river is permitted here and what appears to be a brook on the right has been created from a channel that took waste water to the river from the old Power Station.

To complete the walk, turn right on to the towpath and follow the Thames back to Sonning Bridge. This fine structure, built in 1790 but since strengthened, is worth a special look, as is the Mill, now a theatre and restaurant. Before you leave Sonning, take a look too at the cottages built in 1850 as Alms Houses and at the village pump.

Although some things have changed since Jerome and his friends came to Sonning on their journey along the Thames, a quiet morning, afternoon or evening walk here when the sun is shining still has magic, and not all the changes are for the worse!

LAURENCE BINYON, 1869–1943

THE POETRY OF Laurence Binyon reveals a deep love of nature. As he shows in 'The Cherry Trees', he believes that the beauty of growing things can heal a war-torn world.

> *Out of the dusk of distant woods*
> *All round beneath the April skies*
> *Blossom-white, the cherry trees*
> *Like lovely apparitions rise.*

> *Like spirits strange to this ill world,*
> *White strangers from a world apart,*
> *Like silent promises of peace,*
> *Like hope that blossoms in the heart.*

From 1934 to 1943 Binyon lived at Westridge Farmhouse, close to footpaths that lead up through Streatley Warren to the Ridgeway over the Berkshire Downs. He knew other poets living near by, such

By 1934 Laurence Binyon was a distinguished art historian who for forty years had worked in the British Museum. He had lectured abroad on themes like 'Landscape in English Art and Poetry', and was a leading expert on oriental art. His poetry and plays had been published during these years, as well as a considerable range of art books and articles.

Binyon was born into a Lancaster Quaker family in 1869. His father was a clergyman in a rather poor parish, but there were fond memories of the Yorkshire Dales. After several moves the family settled in London, where Binyon's good Latin earned him a scholarship to St Paul's School. A love of poetry was fostered by aunt Sophia Phillips, and fascination with the culture of India was inspired by school friend Manmohan Ghose. Both were to be strong influences in the future. Binyon's friendship with Ghose continued at Oxford, where other acquaintances included Wilde and Yeats. One of the most useful was Margaret Woods, wife of the Trinity College President, a poet and novelist who was impressed with Binyon's work. She often asked him to their home at Boars Hill, then in rural Berkshire, and in May 1880 he dined there with Robert Bridges who, at forty-five, had just published his *Shorter Poems*. Binyon was invited to stay with the Bridges family at Yattendon and was there shown the poetry of Gerard Manley Hopkins, which would not be published until 1918. The freshness and metrical complexity of the poems made a deep impression on him. During these formative years, rowing on the Thames and walking in the country with friends such as these, in England or abroad, were favoured leisure pursuits.

Binyon began to work in the British Museum in 1893, first in the Reading Room then in 1895 in the Print Room. He built up collections of Japanese and other oriental fine art and published scholarly texts in this field as well as on British art, and William Blake in particular. Always, a quiet, reticent manner hid strong feeling and views, in professional and private life alike. When in 1901 Cicely Powell visited the Print Room, Binyon knew she was his 'dream come true'. She already admired his poetry. Binyon sent long letters, as they tried to resolve some religious differences. In March 1904 he wrote: 'I want to have elemental things near my life. Well love and marriage are that and so is poetry.' They were married in April 1904, and love was the inspiration for many poems written in the years that followed. The last lines of 'Parting and Meeting':

> But when from far in the thronged street
> Our eyes each other leap to find,
> O when at last our arms enwind,
> And on our lips our longings meet,
> The world glows new with each heart-beat,
> Love is come home, Life is enshrined.

Soon twin daughters, Helen and Margaret, were born and in 1911 a third daughter, Nicolete; all three girls grew up to be clever and talented. Relief from family concerns and demanding work came with pleasant days in the country, as depicted by Binyon's carefully crafted poetry. 'Bab-lock-Hythe' tells of 'gliding' in a small boat on the Thames at 'the time of wild roses' past 'High woods, heron-haunted' and 'Old hills greenly mounded'. However, a poet living through the early years of the twentieth century had to come to terms with the horrors of world war, and Binyon also wrote words that spoke, and still speak, for those who mourn and remember. A verse from his poem 'For the Fallen' is inscribed on Lutyen's Cenotaph in Whitehall and has become the core of Remembrance Day services:

They shall grow not old, as we that are left grow old:
Age shall not weary them, nor the years condemn.
At the going down of the sun and in the morning
We will remember them.

The poem was written in September 1914, just after the retreat from Mons, the first battle of the First World War. It is remarkable because it foreshadows much that is to come; it also involves those who stay at home yet suffer and remember. In periods of leave Binyon served as a Red Cross Volunteer in France and Cicely worked in Woolwich Arsenal, while the children stayed with grandparents in the country. Poems written at this time, 'Fetching the Wounded', for instance, showed what war on the front line could mean. In the 1920s, Binyon wrote and edited more poetry and art volumes, and Cicely published books on history; plays were written for Masefield to use in the small Boars Hill theatre. In 1929 a tour of the Far East was at long last arranged, where Binyon gave lectures and saw originals of the prints and paintings he had admired for so long.

In 1933, after a lifetime of service and honour for his accomplishments, Binyon was happy to retire and would, as he had told friends for years, 'write all the poetry schemed ahead of me!' By that time their daughters were independent, so he and Cicely looked for a suitable country home. They found an old farmhouse at Westridge, west of Streatley, surrounded by ancient trackways and earthworks yet remote, under a wide sky. 'The Way Home' expresses Binyon's satisfaction. He speaks of 'the stark form' of a 'tree standing up' 'in stillness and storm', and the poem concludes:

For the thing that is
My comfort is come
Wind washes the plain road:
This is the way home.

Westridge Farm had large neglected gardens, which the Binyons put to good use. They planted hundreds of bulbs, after battling with 'thistle and bindweed'; they renewed an old orchard and grew vegetables. When war began again in 1939 and the Binyon children and grandchildren moved to the farm, the vegetable plot and orchard provided food in plenty. In autumn 1942, for instance, the trees yielded two tons of apples and plums; some produce was sold for the Red Cross, the rest was canned or salted. News

LAURENCE BINYON – WALK 11

Laurence Binyon memorial, St Mary's Church, Aldworth.

from war-torn areas reached Westridge by BBC broadcasts; when there was a bombing raid on London, they could sometimes see anti-aircraft fire from their farm high on the downs. Again, Binyon turned to poetry to try to find hope ; in 'Winter Sunrise' harsh words state:

> ....I see the original fires
> Leaping in spasms, seeking to burst their prison
> And I remember that human eyes have seen
> Solid earth yawn and cities shaken to fragments
> Ocean torn to the bottom and great ships swallowed.

In the final lines the poet returns to his first image, 'the beautiful shadow' of winter jasmine on a 'pale wall'. The madness of 'war in the brain' gives way to the regenerative powers of nature's beauty.

Binyon was still being asked to give lectures in his years at Westridge; three poetry volumes, some plays and art books, and his translations of Dante's *Divine Comedy* were all published during this period; some of the poems are thought to be the finest he ever wrote.

Laurence Binyon died quietly on 10 March 1943 in a Reading nursing home and was buried at Aldworth near Westridge. He and his wife, Cicely, are honoured each Remembrance Day, when poppies are left near the slate memorial slab, sculpted with its flowers and leaves, in St Mary's churchyard, Aldworth.

WALK 11

A LAURENCE BINYON WALK OF FOUR AND A HALF MILES TO THE RIDGEWAY AND ALDWORTH, OR ONE OF THREE MILES TO ALDWORTH

Ordnance Survey Landranger Sheet 174
START POINT: grid reference 565797

WESTRIDGE GREEN, BINYON'S Home village, where this walk begins, is found on the B4009 west of Streatley. Park considerately and take an asphalt farm track that leaves the road to the right of the signpost to Aldworth and walk north-west.

LAURENCE BINYON – WALK 11

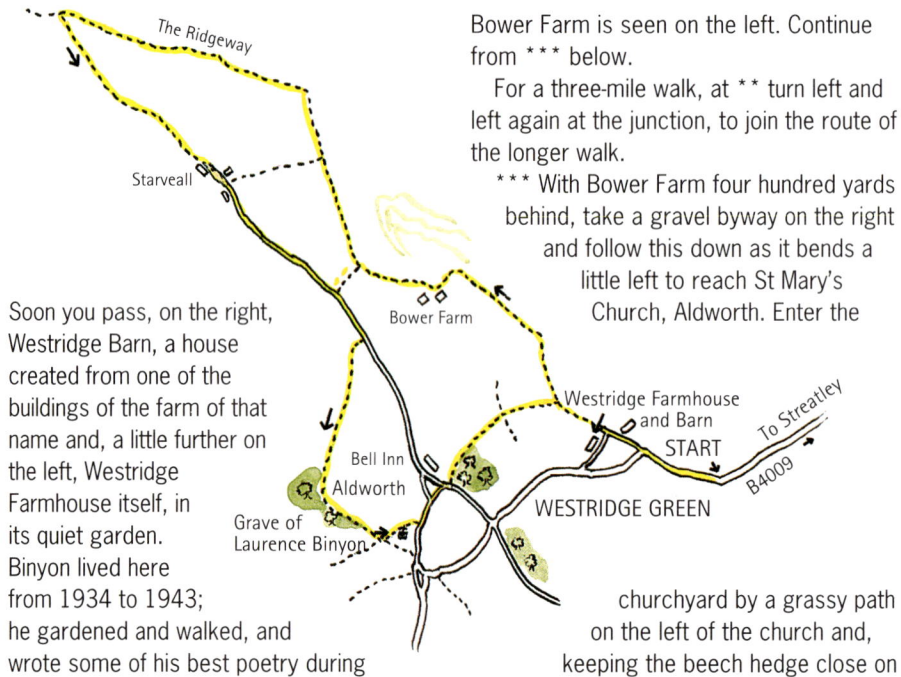

Bower Farm is seen on the left. Continue from *** below.

For a three-mile walk, at ** turn left and left again at the junction, to join the route of the longer walk.

*** With Bower Farm four hundred yards behind, take a gravel byway on the right and follow this down as it bends a little left to reach St Mary's Church, Aldworth. Enter the

Soon you pass, on the right, Westridge Barn, a house created from one of the buildings of the farm of that name and, a little further on the left, Westridge Farmhouse itself, in its quiet garden. Binyon lived here from 1934 to 1943; he gardened and walked, and wrote some of his best poetry during those years.

Walk ahead along the well-marked byway, which becomes a grassy track, and after about half a mile pass through a metal gate. Veer right before the buildings ahead, Bower Farm, ignoring a small stile over the barbed wire fence. Below, on the right, is Streatley Bottom, with ridges marking early field edges, and back further to the north-east there are fine views over the Thames Valley. A gate at the end of the field leads to a track at byway signs.

At this point there is a choice**; either turn right and follow the by-way up to the Ridgeway, as Binyon often did; if you choose this route the walk will be about four and a half miles in all. At the Ridgeway go left and, at the bottom of a slope after about half a mile, turn sharply back left and, ignoring side paths, pass between houses at Starveall and keep ahead until

churchyard by a grassy path on the left of the church and, keeping the beech hedge close on your left, find the grave of Laurence Binyon just beyond a small tree. On a slate slab, decorated with flowers and grasses, are recorded the dates of his life, 1869–1943, and those of his wife Cicely, 1876–1962. Near by is a smaller slab, inscribed Helen Binyon 1904–1979. St Mary's is well-known too for its 'giants', large effigies inside the church of many of the ancient, powerful de la Beche family; details are given of their lives.

To complete the walk, take a path on the right of the church, turn left up the lane and reach The Bell Inn. To the right of the inn turn left and enter a hedged footpath and walk ahead, at first by a hedge on the right then across a small field. Ignoring a cross path, continue ahead to turn right at the byway and again pass Westridge Farm. The Binyons and their visitors would have walked this way often.

JOHN MASEFIELD, 1878–1967

O! to feel the warmth of the rain, and the homely smell of the earth,
Is a tune for the blood to jig to, a joy past power of words;
And the blessed green comely meadows seem all a ripple with mirth
At the lilt of the shifting feet, and the dear wild cry of the birds.

JOHN MASEFIELD'S POEM 'Tewkesbury Road' describes the delight of walking 'Under the flying white clouds and the broad blue lift of the sky'. It was written when he was in his early twenties, as were other much-anthologised poems, for example 'Sea Fever' and 'Cargoes'.

Masefield was born in the small country town of Ledbury in Worcestershire and in his writing he often refers to country walks. His earliest memories were happy ones, but very soon this changed; his mother died when he was six and his solicitor father grew ill because of money problems. When he was twelve, John, with his five brothers and sisters, were made wards of an uncle and aunt, who decided he should be trained as a seaman. John joined the school-ship, *Conway*, in 1891, and by the time he was fifteen he was rounding Cape Horn in the sailing vessel *Gilcruix*. Later he wrote that he knew what it was like to be 'never warm nor dry, nor full nor rested'; experience of forty-foot high seas and 'bows stove in by ice' gave him much to write about later, but at the time proved too much for an untried boy and, with broken nerves, he was sent home.

Already, Masefield planned to be a writer; when he was sent to America to join a second ship, he deserted, took menial work, read extensively and wrote sonnets, which he sent to his sister Ethel. In 1897 he returned to London, where Ethel helped him to find cheap lodgings and a clerk's job. He spent his free time visiting libraries or galleries and writing. He met Yeats, Binyon and other writers, and his poems began to appear in magazines. By 1914, when he first came to live in Berkshire, he had become a well-known and respected poet; *Salt Water Ballads* and other books of poetry had been published, plays, such as *The Campden Wonder*, had been produced at the Court Theatre and magazine articles had appeared. By then he had been married to Constance for eleven years and had two children, Judith, aged ten, and Lewis, aged four.

Masefield did not lose his love of wild beauty during his years in London and often escaped to the country. In spring 1903, for instance, he visited Jack Yeats and his wife in their Devon home; he took books to review but there was also time for some walks of twenty miles or so. He wrote to Constance: 'We stand on a great hillside...and have gorse in full bloom above and below a fine wood...a faint smell of woodsmoke with a strong smell of primroses and wet grass...'.

JOHN MASEFIELD

The Masefields found their own homes in the country and retreated to them from city life. First, in 1909, they took a 'farm in Buckinghamshire high up on a chalk hill, surrounded by beechwoods'. Then, in 1914, a move to Lollingdon Farm, which was centuries old, moated and on the edge of the Berkshire Downs, gave them even more pleasure. They climbed Lollingdon Hill and Masefield wrote to his brother Harry 'one is said to be able to walk for forty miles on grass to Old Sarum gates'. Rupert Brooke and Violet Asquith, among other friends, visited and wandered on the downs with the family and found 'it was a good bird and flower place'.

In these years, Masefield derived poetic inspiration from the land in the way he had done from the sea earlier in his life. Usually he wrote out of doors; Constance recalled that 'he left Lollingdon Farm, his working book in his pocket, and no matter how cold it was, sat and thought and saw the big world in his imagination'. He had much to think about as news of the war reached the quiet downland villages; in *August, 1914* he wrote:

> *These homes, this valley spread below me here,*
> *The rooks, the tilted stacks, the beasts in pen,*
> *Have been the heartfelt things, past-speaking dear*
> *To unknown generations of dead men,*

These, he continued, had left their farms when called on to defend their country knowing what neglect of the fields and trackways would mean:-

> *The harvest not yet won, the empty bin,*
> *The friendly horses taken from the stalls,*
> *The fallow on the hill not yet brought in,*
> *The cracks unplastered in the leaking walls.*

> *Yet heard the news and went discouraged home,*
> *And brooded by the fire with heavy mind*
> *With such dumb loving of the Berkshire loam*
> *As breaks the dumb hearts of the English kind.*

> *They sadly rose and left the well-loved Downs,*
> *And so by ship to sea, and knew no more*
> *The fields of home, the byres, the market towns,*
> *Nor the dear outline of the English shore.*

Cavalry and their horses were billeted at Lollingdon Farm for a while, so the Masefields moved to London. Soon, however, they returned to live off the land as far as possible, and they walked across the fields to Wallingford for supplies. Masefield, now too old for the army, wrote some of his most thoughtful poetry as he attempted to come to terms with the evil of war. In *Lollingdon Downs and Other Poems, with Sonnets*, he tried to examine where beauty and faith in the future can be found, in a world in tumult. Spurred by conscience to more active war work, early in 1915 Masefield went to France as a Red Cross field orderly; when medical duties were done, he wrote to Constance about the suffering and sadness. He thought a travelling field unit could get closer to the front, to treat the badly wounded men, so when he was on leave he raised money from friends to set one up. He also toured France to assess medical needs, went to Gallipoli for the Red Cross and to America to lecture about the war. In between he retired to Hampstead or Lollingdon to write of his experiences; his prose work *Gallipoli*, published in 1916, was received with interest in France and America as well as in Britain.

In 1917 the Masefields moved from moated Lollingdon Farm to a drier redbrick

JOHN MASEFIELD

Lollingdon Farmhouse.

house called Hill Crest, on Boars Hill. Nearer to Oxford, but still in Berkshire then, the house had fine views, south to the downs and north over Oxford. Constance wrote 'though we haven't the dear walk up Lollingdon Hill, we have very pure fresh air, and a jolly scent of gorse and bracken'. Robert Bridges had built a house at Boars Hill and, when war ended, the area became home to more celebrities. There was a cottage in their wooded garden where Robert Graves, his wife Nancy and baby girl lived for more than a year; another neighbour was Edmund Blunden who, after recuperating – like Graves – from shell-shock, was Professor of Poetry at Oxford.

During the 1920s Masefield wrote on a range of themes, in a variety of forms – the children's classic *Midnight Fox*, for instance. He shared his delight in drama and poetry-speaking with Oxford undergraduates and local people alike, and the Masefields played a full part in promoting cultural activities. The village hall, in nearby Wooton, was hired for amateur productions of plays such as Euripides' *Hippolytus* and the *Pot of Broth* by Yeats; Masefield was producer, Constance wardrobe and property person, and daughter Judith an ardent and striking actress. By 1924 a small theatre, which became known as the Music Room, was built on land next door to Hillcrest. The Hill Players presented plays in this pleasant little theatre, whose good acoustics did them full justice. Performances included *Hamlet*, Yeats' *Deirdre* and verse dramas by Masefield himself.

Convinced that poetry should be spoken not read silently, Masefield set up the Oxford Recitations. By 1929 he lost interest in the competitive nature of these and they gave way to festivals; his claim that poetry be spoken 'beautifully' influenced many during future years. His plays on religious subjects, such as *The Coming of Christ*, performed in Canterbury Cathedral, were written during the Boars Hill years, along with lectures on literary subjects and some poetry.

Oxford University made John Masefield Honorary Doctor of Literature in 1922, in the 1930s he received the Order of Merit from George V and more honours from universities on both sides of the Atlantic and, when Bridges died, he became Poet Laureate.

As the years went by, Masefield never lost a yearning to be out in the country. A field was added to the garden at Hill Crest, and when visitors to the new Poet Laureate asked if he wrote out of doors he replied 'Always, whenever I can, until the rain makes the ink run, or the frost freezes it on my pen.' Constance became ill in 1932, so they moved, first to a house in Pinsbury Park in the Cotswolds, which proved cold in winter, then back to Clifton Hampden, on the Oxfordshire side of the Thames. The lawn at Burcote Brook ran down to the river, there were acres of tangled woodland, 'tall trees with a rookery, willows where kingfishers flashed and thickets where nightingales nested', and the poet kept a view across Berkshire: he wrote 'We look out on the river and on Wittenham Clumps.'

Masefield lived quietly, still writing, into his late eighties; he died at Clifton Hampden in 1967, when he was eighty-nine. His expressed wish, that his ashes be scattered in the open air, was not fulfilled; instead he has an honoured place in Poet's Corner, Westminster Abbey. Constance had died earlier, in her ninety-third year, and his novelist son, Lewis, had died during the Second World War. The passage of time, with inevitable losses but some gain, is the theme of a late poem, *On Growing Old*:

Be with me, Beauty, for the fire is dying;
My dog and I are old, too old for roving...
I cannot sail your seas, I cannot wander
Your cornland, nor your hill-land, nor your valleys
Ever again, nor share the battle yonder...
Only stay quiet while my mind remembers
The beauty of fire from the beauty of embers.

The activities of his early days, sailing and rambling in the country, about which he wrote so vigorously in his youth, have left memories for an old man to treasure. So too for us, the walkers who trace his footsteps.

Walk 12 on John Masefield follows the section below on Agatha Christie as it includes a visit to her grave.

AGATHA CHRISTIE, 1890–1976

AGATHA CHRISTIE, THOUGH writing in a different genre, is included in this chapter with John Masefield as her grave in Cholsey is near Lollingdon Farm and both can be visited on the same walk.

JOHN MASEFIELD – WALK 12

Agatha Christie moved to Berkshire at the end of the 1914–18 war. After her marriage in 1914 she had worked as a VAD nurse while her colonel husband served in France. When they were re-united they bought a house in Sunningdale, naming it Styles after Agatha's first published book. The couple were well-off compared to many, but the war had changed them, and their marriage did not last. Archibald Christie moved out, and Agatha then caused much publicity by apparently disappearing, even though she had only retreated to a quiet hotel in Harrogate.

The steady production of Poirot books continued and in 1930 Miss Marple made her first appearance in *Murder at the Vicarage*. Much of Agatha Christie's writing is set in the villages and country houses that she knew so well. After she had married archaeologist Max Mallowan, however, travel to exotic locations began to feature in her books. At Queen Mary's request, she wrote a radio play, which was later adapted for the stage. *The Mousetrap*, as this play became, has run continuously since 1952. The play has one stage-set, the Great Hall of Monkswell Manor, in Berkshire, where the characters are cut off by snow and need a sledge to reach Newbury.

The popularity of Agatha Christie's work does not diminish. New films continue to be made from her mysteries, and the books are translated into many languages. During her lifetime she received numerous honours; she was made Dame of the British Empire in 1971. She died in 1976 and is buried in the quiet churchyard of St Mary Birinus at Cholsey.

WALK 12

A JOHN MASEFIELD WALK OF FIVE MILES FROM ASTON TIRROLD, WHICH ALSO VISITS THE GRAVE OF AGATHA CHRISTIE

Ordnance Survey Landranger Sheet 174
START POINT: grid reference 557861

BEGIN THIS WALK near St Michael's Church, to the east of the lovely village of Aston Tirrold. Find Aston Tirrold four miles north-west of Streatley, off the A417 to Wantage.

With your back to the church, walk left fifty yards, and enter a path on the right. Cross a stile ahead, then walk diagonally left to a stile and enter a field ahead through a farm gate and turn right, along a concrete track that skirts the hedge on your right. Cross two stiles and continue ahead to the end of a fence on the left; here turn left and walk forward to pass under power lines.

Turn right before a ditch and keeping this on your left reach a metal-railed footbridge on the left and cross this. Turning a little left, see Cholsey Church ahead; follow the path towards it over the railway bridge, then four hundred yards before Manor Farm turn right across the field to reach the churchyard and a stile into it.

81

JOHN MASEFIELD – WALK 12

The grave of Agatha Christie and Max Mallowan lies ahead by the wall on the left and is marked by a large headstone. A plaque on the wall shows that in 1990 twenty-five trees were planted near by in her memory; these are growing well and will increasingly add beauty and shade to the spot. In about 1171 the solid Norman church, St Mary's, was built by monks whose earlier monastery had been destroyed by the Danes. Manor Farm once had a medieval tithe barn, England's largest, twice as large as the one north of Great Coxwell.

Farm, where the Masefields lived; it is quiet still, and in February pretty with snowdrops.

To reach the hill, where Masefield went to think and write or the family took visiting friends to see the views, walk back along the farm track for a few yards and opposite outbuildings take a wide path on the right, which climbs and circles Lollingdon Hill. As you climb, ignore what seems to be a path on the right; keep to the main track until it is over the brow of the hill then, after a fence, turn right along grass by the side of a field, with the fence on your right. Go through a gate ahead and take a footpath from this corner of the field down diagonally to the right to reach the lower track again. Turn left and shortly take a wide path that forks from the track; continue on this until you reach the path by which you left the village. Turn left into this and left again to reach the start.

Leave the churchyard by a stile in the southern wall, cross the field a little to the right and go over two stiles in its corner. With the railway branch line on your left, reach a stile and footbridge. Do not take the tunnel on the left but veer right to take a tunnel under the main line. Now take a stile to the left and cross a paddock diagonally to the right and cross a footbridge. Walk ahead for a mile or so, passing a pylon, and reach a farm road. Here turn right and, soon, on the right and set back from the track, see moated Lollingdon

82

EDWARD THOMAS, 1878–1917

CHARACTERISED BY LYRICAL simplicity, Edward Thomas's poetry often speaks of the beauty of nature; *Thaw*, for example, in just four lines, captures a certain time of the year quite magically:

> *Over the land freckled with snow half-thawed*
> *The speculating rooks at their nests cawed*
> *And saw from the elm tops, delicate*
> *as flower of grass,*
> *What we below could not see, Winter pass.*

As a boy, Thomas loved books by naturalists and on country lore; later, these interests would predominate in his poetry and prose. His writing shows, too, that he often walked thirty miles between dawn and dusk, considering 'a lost footpath on a map or in reality as a challenge'. His visits to Berkshire, when he was researching his book on the Icknield Way, for example, did not last more than a few days at a time, but he quite literally put some of the paths of this county on the map, so he cannot be left out.

Edward Thomas did not always find life easy; in *It Rains* he says:

> *And I am nearly as happy as possible*
> *To search the wilderness in vain though well,*
> *To think of two walking, kissing there,*
> *Drenched, yet forgetting the kisses of the rain:*

The poem then says '…never, never again, / Unless alone' will he find happiness in a walk in the rain. A later letter claimed 'I always walk alone', but he did at times enjoy a meeting with other travellers – like Lob, whose face was 'rough, brown, sweet as any nut'. 'The man was wild and wandered/His home was where he was free.' Lob had advice for him:

> *Nobody can't stop 'ee. It's*
> *A footpath right enough.*

Fascinated by paths, tracks and roads, Thomas set out to trace the prehistoric Icknield Way and write a book about it. He writes 'It is one of the adventurous pleasures of a good map thus to trace the possible course of a known old road or to discover one that was lost'. He says that a distinct chain of road, lane and footpath, especially if it follows a boundary, is likely to be an ancient way. For his book on the Icknield Way, Thomas made notes for nine days in the British Museum, and then walked routes for ten days, mostly in the Berkshire of 1915.

The two most likely routes for the Icknield Way were the Ridgeway and a lower road about five miles to the north. As early as 1695, Wise, in his *Antiquities of Berkshire*, favoured the lower route and Thomas, as he walked and collected evidence, had little doubt that the ancient roadway could be clearly traced and much of it was still being used by ramblers.

Although it was not his first choice, Thomas did spend two days walking along the Ridgeway west of Streatley for, as he said, he 'liked it'; from Streatley he rambled to Scutchamer Knob, the Devil's Punchbowl, Whitehorse Hill and Wayland's Smithy. For the next two days, he explored the lower route, assuming that the Way would have crossed the Thames near Streatley again. After curving north, on what is now the A417, he tried a way from Upton, past Hagbourne Hill and Aldfield Common to East Lockinge and then West Lockinge. No path across Lockinge Park appears to have survived, but the route continued south of Wantage, passing by The Mead, the Betjeman family home, through Childrey, Sparshot and beyond. It was also likely that the Icknield Way crossed the Thames further north near Wallingford, so Thomas explored tracks from Watlington to Upton, by way of Ewelme.

Thomas could clearly see possible routes on his maps, and they are also evident on today's Ordnance Survey maps. Local memory of the use of the name Icknield, or variations of it, for some tracks was added proof. In prose, Thomas described what he passed:

Below on the left, were the steep walls of the winding coombe, dotted by thorn, juniper and elder, and here called Streatley Warren. Of the unwooded coombes or inlets to the downs this is one of the most pleasing to me; I shall always remember it, as I do...others of those vast turf halls which the sky roofs.

His poetry too, as in 'Over the Hills', recalls his walks on the Berkshire Downs.

Often and often it came back again
To mind, the day I passed the horizon ridge
To a new country, the path I had to find
By half gaps that were stiles once in the hedge,
The pack of scarlet clouds running across
The harvest evening that seemed endless then.

Thomas left records that allow us to walk with knowledge and pleasure. His poetic journey unfinished, he died fighting near Arras in France in 1917. His wife, Helen, spent her last years in Eastbury, a small village five miles north of Hungerford. There is a memorial window to Edward and Helen in its church; it is engraved by Laurence Whistler in clear glass with scenes of hills, sea and trees, interspersed with lines from his poetry.

Memorial window to Edward Thomas, engraved by Laurence Whistler, in St James the Greater Church, Eastbury.

EDWARD THOMAS – WALK 13

WALK 13

AN EDWARD THOMAS WALK OF ALMOST TEN MILES, ALONG SOME OF THE ICKNIELD WAY AND THE RIDGEWAY

Ordnance Survey Landranger Sheet 174
START POINT: grid reference 479840

THE WALK DESCRIBED here is circular and just less than ten miles long. It does not completely follow the walks Edward Thomas made in Berkshire, but covers parts of both the Icknield Way and the Ridgeway. Begin from the car park at Bury Down on the Ridgeway, where there is also a Ridgeway Explorer bus stop. Bury Down is on a minor road off the A34, a mile south of Chilton or a mile north of West Ilsley.

Leave Bury Down by walking along the Ridgeway to the south-east. After about half a mile, follow the Ridgeway under the A34. The traffic noise has grown since 1915; luckily it does not last for long! To help walkers ignore it, there is a mural in the underpass depicting the history of the Compton Hundred villages from 3000 BC in action pictures and amusing verse.

Immediately on emerging from the underpass, take a signposted public bridleway to the left and, after 150 yards, a stile on the right; cross the track and the stile opposite. Cross a field corner diagonally left, to a stile in the fence ahead and walk down the next field, keeping to the right side. On reaching the hedge, over a rather overgrown Grim's Ditch, look for a stile on the far side of the bushes about twenty five yards from their right end; cross this, two fields, a track and a further field ahead, moving away from the noise of the A34.

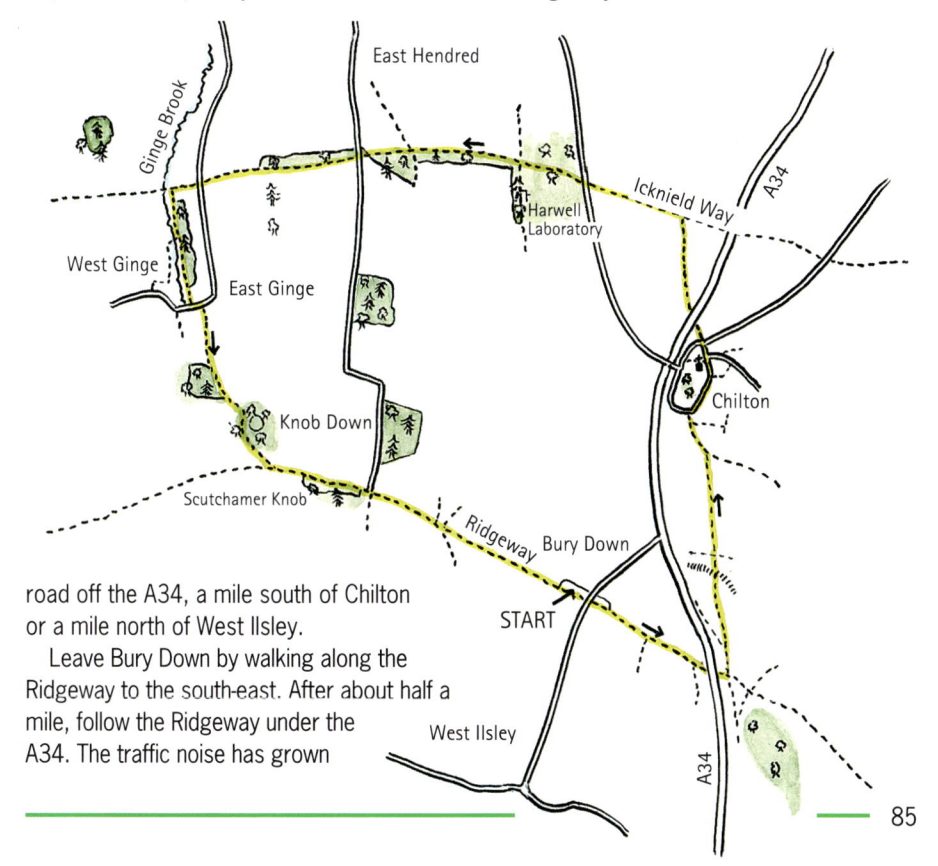

When the path joins a hedged byway, turn left and walk ahead, ignoring a path on the right, to reach Chilton village. Keep ahead, past the Rose and Crown, to the small village green and its pump. Turn a little left, up Church Hill, to reach All Saints Church, some parts of which date from the twelfth century. From the church, walk on to cross roads; here, take the drive ahead on the right of a big farm building. Follow this drive to pass under the A34 and then walk ahead on a gravel track, to reach what is accepted as the Icknield Way.

Edward Thomas was sure this was the ancient route he was looking for; he reports 'Roman things' had been dug up at Hagbourne Hill, visible to the right as we join the Way. Our walk turns left on the wide straight path and, after crossing a busy road, continues ahead on a bridleway skirting Harwell Laboratory. This establishment did not exist, of course, in Thomas's day but the route is marked by numerous signs naming it 'Icknield or Ickleton Way'. Follow the signs round left, then turn right through a fenced path and cross an old track, Hungerford Road, which is mentioned by Thomas. Keep ahead to pass Aldfield Farm and Common, and about a mile beyond Harwell see a path to the right; this is Cow Lane, which, at the end of a ninth day of walking, took Thomas to East Hendred. To the noise of 'rain dripping steadily off the inn roof' he was told by 'an intelligent, unprejudiced' local man that the field-way he had followed was Ickleton Street or Ickleton Meer.

Continue west to a road ahead, where a short way along on the right is a house called Icknield; cross the road and keep ahead passing Park Hill on your right. Cross another small road and with the hedge on your left follow a Right of Way sign until the path descends. Turn left before the stream. Thomas said that 'little Ginge Brook and its hollow of elms and ash trees interrupted the road': he was walking west, on the Icknield Way, however, and soon passed Roundabout Hill. We leave the Way and walk upstream, keeping Ginge Brook on our right. The brook is fed by springs, watercress grows in some spots, and halfway up there is a small waterfall. Pass West Ginge, which lies on the opposite bank, and cross a stile to reach East Ginge.

At a small road go left for a hundred yards, then right at a Right of Way sign near a post box. This path climbs up for about a mile, curving a little to the left, past clumps of trees on Knob Down and over a field. Reach the Ridgeway through a gate. Turn left and soon come to Scutchamer Knob, on your right. 'In one of the roadside woods', wrote Thomas, 'a great tumulus stood disembowelled among the beeches.' Continue along the Ridgeway, following signs carefully at path junctions and complete the walk at Bury Down.

It would not be difficult to follow Edward Thomas's routes from one side of Old Berkshire to the other using Ordnance Survey Pathfinder Sheet 1155. Begin from Aston Tirrold, Grid Reference 554859, for the Icknield Way route. Thomas's book *The Icknield Way* explains the lower route from Streatley to Ashbury fairly well, and the Ridgeway, the higher route, is signposted at each junction. Walks 5, 11, 15 and 16 in this book also cover sections of the higher route. Thomas describes some of the inns he stayed in; he says less about how he travelled to and from walks. If you wish to try these longer walks, public transport to the start and from the finish may still be possible.

DAVID HERBERT LAWRENCE, 1885–1930

Here the woods are all yellow – big, yellow woods. I never saw them more lovely. The other day we went getting chestnuts. There were quite a number. This is a pleasant place.

SO WROTE DH LAWRENCE on 30 October 1918 from Chapel Farm Cottage, Hermitage, near Newbury, Berkshire.

DH Lawrence lived in Berkshire for most of the period from December 1917 to November 1919. He is well known for his novels and poetry but he also wrote plays, short stories, essays, travel books and many letters. He is now thought of as a major literary figure, but in the early years of the twentieth century he did not find it easy to gain publication for his radical views and outspoken description. He came to Hermitage with his German wife, Frieda, for several reasons. In 1917, while living near St Ives in Cornwall, he sent several urgent letters; in one he wrote: 'Sudden blow! we are served with notice to leave the area of Cornwall by Monday next, ... by the military. It is a complete mystery to me – complete.'

DH Lawrence, exempted from fighting because of his poor health, openly antagonistic to war, and with a German wife, was regarded as suspicious and it was advisable to live away from the coast, quietly in the country. The couple were lent a tiny cottage in Hermitage by Margaret Radford, daughter of a sympathetic friend. Next door lived a family whose daughter, Hilda, later recalled those days. She spoke of 'many visits from the police', so even in Hermitage, they were not left in peace. Lawrence spent hours writing 'at incredible speed' but he also grew vegetables, sketched and painted, checked Hilda's homework and explored the woods and surrounding fields. Hilda reports:

He used to walk many miles; often he would leave home in the morning and not return until late in the afternoon. After tea some evenings we walked from the farm across the fields and out on Cold Ash Common, from which there was a wonderful view across the village and beyond. I am sure that Mr Lawrence enjoyed all those walks; the beauty of the surroundings and the glorious panorama of colour, which on those summer evenings extended right to the hills on the distant horizon.

Others tell of walks that Lawrence took; Joan Thornycroft Fargeon, sister-in-law of the poetess Eleanor, had a house, Spring Cottage, on Bucklebury Common and writes of her first meeting with

87

Lawrence: 'He had walked over from his cottage in Hermitage, about five miles away, ... He came walking up our drive, holding a small bouquet of wild flowers he had gathered along the way, and looking like a Christ-figure with his red hair and beard.'

In July 1919 Douglas Goldring was interested in producing Lawrence's play *Touch and Go* in a Peoples' Theatre Society. He visited Hermitage and wrote: 'I may mention that to go for a walk with Lawrence through the English countryside, was an unforgettable experience. Lawrence made me feel that I had never really "seen" a wood before.'

Very few other authors reveal such a close knowledge of wild flowers, trees, birds and landscape features as Lawrence. He used description, imagery and allusion to convey a sense of place and his own intense response to wherever he was living and what he was seeing. In letters, he described the Berkshire countryside to his friends. On 16 February 1918 he ended his letter to Catherine Carswell: 'There are primroses in the wood – and avenues of yellow catkins, hanging like curtains.' On 12 March 1918 he explained to William Hopkin: 'It is very nice here, Hardy country – like *Woodlanders* – all woods and hazel copses, and tiny villages that will sleep for ever.' Then on 28 April 1918, to Catherine, he again wrote: 'This evening we went through the woods and I found a dead owl at my feet, a lovely soft warm-brown thing. Also we found some very lovely big cowslips, whose scent is really a communication direct from the source of creation.'

Even when unwell, Lawrence found solace in studying the quiet world he saw from his bedroom window; 17 January 1918, he wrote to Cecil Gray: 'As the evening falls, and it is snowy, there is a clear yellow light, an evening star and a moon. The trees get dark. Those without leaves seem to thrill their twigs above, the firs and pines slant heavy with snow.'

In Lawrence's novels and poetry, the natural world acts as a setting against which the emotions and actions of the characters are developed. The title of Chapter 1, Part Two of *The White Peacock* is 'Strange New Budding'; nature in springtime symbolises burgeoning young love:

So we went along by the hurrying brook which fell over little cascades in its haste, never looking once at the primroses that were glimmering along its banks. We came to the top of a slope where the wood thinned. As I talked to Emily I became dimly aware that...the ground was white with snowdrops, like drops of manna scattered over the red earth...

Later in the novel, a description of the meadows in June intensifies the expression of heightened feelings:

Little early birds fluttered in and out of the foamy meadow-sea, dashing past the crimson sorrel cresset. Under the froth of flowers were the purple vetch clumps, yellow milk vetches, and the pink of the wood betony and the floating stars of marguerites. There was a weight of honeysuckle on the hedges, where pink roses were waking up for their broadspread flight through the day.

These are just short passages from typically lavish descriptions of the natural world, by which Lawrence enriches his themes; yet they remind us of the beauty

DAVID HERBERT LAWRENCE

Chapel Farm Cottage, Hermitage.

of the countryside around Hermitage, beauty that walkers can still find.

Of all Lawrence's writing, the story most closely based on Hermitage is 'The Fox', first published in 1923 in *Three Novellas*. The story takes place at Bailey Farm. Two women work the farm, without help until a young soldier returns to the home he had shared with his grandfather. Finding that the old man has died and there are no free lodgings in the village, he stays. The actual farm on which this fictional one was based was Grimsbury Farm, in Long Lane, Hermitage. The Lawrences became friends with Cecily Lambert Minchin who, with her friend Violet Monk, had been staying with her grandfather and after his death had had to take over the work of the farm. Cecily's memoir records their first meeting:

> It was nearly dark when they arrived...we had just been in the throes of milking goats, feeding pigs and hens and were tired out from a long day's uncongenial work and not...in a fit state mentally or physically, clogged as we were with farmyard muck, to greet and entertain strange visitors. However we invited them in, lit a fire in our best parlour for their benefit, made some tea, and sat down to a meal of bread and jam – all we had to offer at that time. It was during the war when things were short and we were desperately poor, being complete novices at the farm game.

89

Later this hospitality was returned; Frieda entertained, while Lawrence cooked a 'rich stew with mushrooms and potatoes smothered with butter'.

Although Cecily Minchin felt the events, and relationships, in 'The Fox' bore little relation to the real lives of the two women, almost all of the detail in the passage above finds a place in the story. The setting with the farm house and its outbuildings, the fields and nearby woods, and the railway that ran close by, are all recreated accurately. The nearby market town is clearly Newbury, and from their windows 'the wide country stretches hollow and dim to the round hills of the White Horse'.

Cecily Minchin's own description of Violet Monk, her appearance, manner and Land Girl's uniform are all close to Lawrence's depiction of Nellie March; Violet's 'dark wavy hair and velvety brown eyes' become in March 'crisp dark hair' and 'big and wide and handsome' eyes; the boyish but graceful figure, the shy yet sardonic manner were observed by the writer and became the material he worked with. Cecily Minchin's parents stayed at the the farm, as did her brother on sick leave from the army; soldiers were also billeted in the village.

In the novella, Banford's parents stay at Bailey Farm and the depiction of Henry Grenfel, the fictional young soldier, is reminiscent of real young men on leave. Although the main events and relationships in 'The Fox' differ from those recorded in the memoirs, close knowledge of life at Grimsbury Farm supplied setting and much material for the characters. Lawrence and Frieda even spent two weeks with Cecily Minchin and Violet Monk in 1919, when Chapel Farm Cottage was needed by the Radfords; with this insight, the author adapted and developed his narrative and themes.

The Lawrences lived in another Berkshire house for the month of August 1919; Rosalind Baynes lent them Myrtle Cottage, in Pangbourne. They loved the house and especially the fruit orchard in its pleasant gardens, but there were too many people in Pangbourne for Lawrence, who preferred 'tramping the Downs above Streatley'. Hilda, the Lawrences' neighbour in Hermitage, remembers such a day in her school holidays when, carrying meals with them, they climbed among gorse and at the top 'paused to admire the glorious view of the River Thames winding its way through the valley'. The plan was to walk to Compton but they did not get that far:

> We walked for many miles, taking our bearings by the sun. We saw many sheep; apart from them, one shepherd with his dog, the birds, and the rabbits, we were the only creatures around. We revelled in the quiet beauty which we had all to ourselves. We had our meal on the side of a hill and watched the birds circling overhead.

They turned back in late afternoon; the tired youngsters asked 'Uncle' Lawrence how much further it was and he replied 'Only round the corner, if we ever get to the damn thing!' Even keen walkers sometimes tire! On 6 November 1919 Lawrence wrote his last letter from Chapel Farm in Hermitage to Catherine Carswell: 'I am preparing to go to Italy – selling my books in Reading...' Frieda had gone to Baden, to visit relatives, before joining him there.

DAVID HERBERT LAWRENCE – WALK 14

Apart from 'The Fox', while he was in Berkshire Lawrence worked on novels, literary criticism and poetry. A large part of *Aaron's Rod* was written between 1917 and 1919; just the last chapters of the novel were set and completed in Italy. *Studies in Classic American Literature*, *Movements in European History*, and *The Reality of Peace* were all written as far as first draft stage at least. He carried out some revision of earlier work, including *Women in Love*, and short stories, such as *The Blind Man*, and a play *Touch and Go*, also date from the years in Hermitage. To earn much-needed money, Lawrence prepared earlier poems for publication. He sold a small group outright for £10 to make a limited edition called *Bay*. He wrote to Lady Cynthia Asquith on 26 September 1918: 'Your poems will come before Christmas meanwhile Secker is bringing out a little 2/6d volume almost immediately called *New Poems*. I'll give it you when it comes. Your *Bay* will be thin, about 20 pieces in it – but hand-printed and beautiful, 7/6d.' *New Poems* was published in October 1918, *Bay* in November 1919; also that year, a first edition of Lawrence's *Collected Poems* was being planned. The quiet years spent in Berkshire produced some fine writing.

WALK 14

A DH LAWRENCE WALK OF FIVE AND A HALF MILES IN AND AROUND HERMITAGE

Ordnance Survey Landranger Sheet 174
START POINT: grid reference 509731

DH LAWRENCE AND Frieda travelled on foot or by train. This walk passes places they knew well and several times crosses the railway line they and their friends used. It is between five and six miles long; if you would prefer a three-mile walk, at * continue along the road, Wellhouse Lane, into Marlston Road and rejoin the main walk at **.
Begin the walk in Hermitage from The Fox, an appropriately named inn, where it may be possible to park. Hermitage is on the B4009, five miles north-east of Newbury.
Some parts of The Fox were built in 1635, as farm cottages; just before Lawrence came to

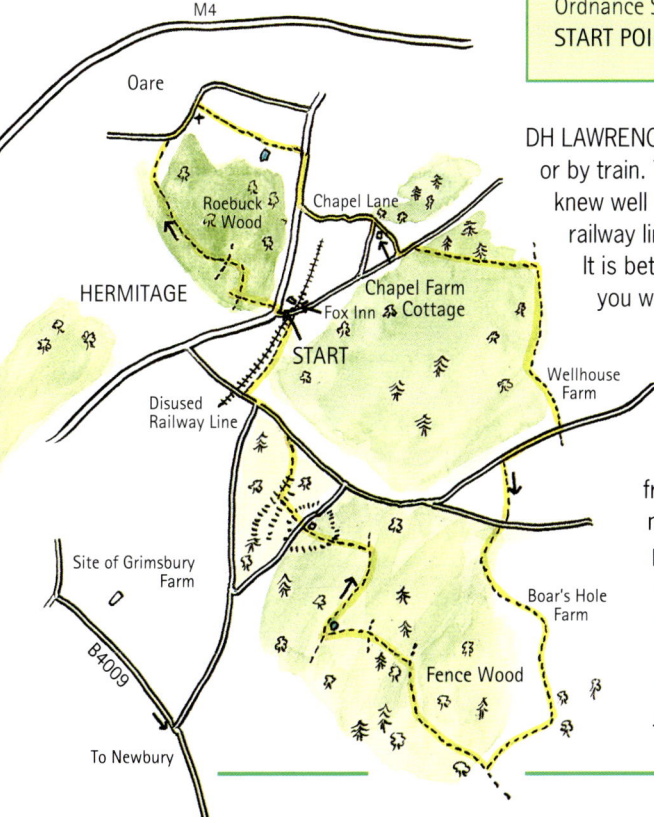

91

Hermitage, the property was enlarged to form an inn. Its name was probably chosen before Lawrence's tale was written and, as other nearby pub names include 'Fox', we can assume the animal was a common sight locally.

Facing the front of the pub, take the fenced path across the road on the left, level with the inn sign. Enter Roebuck Wood and take the winding path that leads up through the wood. When you reach a small cross path, turn right and walk to a path junction; here turn left and keep to this wider path, crossing earthworks and going as straight ahead as possible.

Reach a grassy space with a seat and continue ahead, on a path in line with the seat, to pass a waymark post and reach another open space with a house on the left. Turn right at the next signpost and follow a path, which leads down through woods to reach a road at Oare.

On one of the occasions when the Lawrences had to vacate Chapel Farm Cottage, they stayed in Oare. This small village was once proud of its important priory; now the M4 is very close and it has lost the peace it must have known for centuries. Even in Lawrence's day it must have been quiet.

Turn right, to reach St Bartholomew's Church, built on the site of the priory's chapel and well worth a visit; Oare's history from AD 968 is outlined inside the church. The priory, except for 'the people's church', was destroyed by Henry VIII, but its history lives on in local names like Chapel Lane and Chapel Farm Cottage, where the Lawrences lived.

Turn right after Oare Cottage, cross a stile into Chapel Meadow, passing the remains of the pond where the monks bred carp and keeping the hedge on your left. Cross another stile, then bear left to reach the road. Turn right to pass a school, then take the second road on the left, which is Chapel Lane. Walk along it over a bridge that used to span the railway. At the second turning on the right you reach Chapel Farm Cottage; it is the first house on the left, with its front entrance in Pond Lane and its rear garden backing on to Chapel Lane. The cottage was divided between two families in 1919; now, although the two parts appear to be joined to form one home set in a pleasant garden, its structure seems unchanged and one can picture the Lawrences and their visitors in the garden under the apple trees.

The walk continues along Chapel Lane, in the direction of Grimsbury Farm. The farmhouse, which was the setting of the story 'The Fox', no longer exists and busy roads cross the path the Lawrences would have taken when making a visit to Cecily Minchin and Violet Monk. We can follow some of the way, however, so continue down Chapel Lane to reach the Yattendon Road and turn left. Ignore the first path but after 400 yards or so enter the wood on the right at a footpath sign.

Follow a wide path through woods to a T-junction; here turn right and take this track, passing Wellhouse Farm on the left. At the road * ignore a byway sign opposite; turn right and take the second byway on the left. At the next road, cross over and follow the tarmac drive past Boar's Hole Farm. Continue until you reach the top of the hill with woods on your left and views of the country towards Newbury, much as described by Hilda.

Before the path veers left, go through a signposted gate on the right, go across a field to a metal gate opposite and walk ahead to where paths join. Turn hard right, through a metal gate, on to a bridleway into Fence Wood. Walk ahead on this wide track, for about half a mile, ignoring paths on the left until you reach the far end of a plantation of young Christmas, cherry and birch trees. Here turn left up a grassy path. At a staggered junction walk ahead up a rising path. You pass Fence Pond on your right, but note that in dry weather this will be difficult to see, as it turns into a dry hollow. After the pond, reach a wider path and turn right. Continue to where a stream passes under the track; here turn left up a path by conifers. At the next junction turn right and climb to a (probably welcome!) seat, and turn left to reach the top of the hill. Go left of a turreted house, called Grimsbury Castle because it lies on the site of an Iron Age fort. In 1918 the fields of Grimsbury Farm lay beyond this house. The site of the farmhouse on Red Shute Hill, to the west, is now occupied by Dalton's Mill, an Animal Feeds firm.

To complete the walk, cross the road, go into the trees and across an earthwork ditch ahead. Turn right along the top of a second bank; where this ends, walk downhill through trees and reach Marlston Road. Walk to the left and ** just before the railway arch turn right to follow a path below the embankment, which once carried the railway. This is now used as a play area by Hermitage youngsters. When the path reaches the road turn left to return to the starting point.

Records show Lawrence and Frieda lived in two Pangbourne houses, each for a few weeks, when Chapel Cottage was not free. The Myrtles, lent to them by Rosalind Baynes, seems likely to be 38 Reading Road, which was subsequently known as Myrtle Grove and now Kylemore. The second house can be found on Shooters Hill, the Thames-side road to Streatley from Pangbourne. Called Cliffdene, it is part of the first of the Victorian villas known as the Seven Deadly Sins. The second of the Kenneth Grahame walks, Walk 9, passes these houses, which in Lawrence's time were summer homes for the wealthy.

JOHN BETJEMAN, 1906–1984

JOHN BETJEMAN SPEAKS for walkers in a special way. Whether he writes of the London where he was born, the Oxford where he was educated, the Cornwall of his early holidays, or the Berkshire Downs of his married years, he creates a sense of place. He pictures the history that he feels should not be lost, and writes of the work and lives that have shaped the landscape.

Betjeman was born in Highgate, north London, in 1906; he was an only child in supportive family circumstances. In *Summoned by Bells* he recalls the horse-drawn trams, the family's brougham, the lively neighbours and his best friend, his teddy, Archibald. At his first school, Byron House, he remembers his 'first and purest love, Miss Purey-Cust':

> *Satchel on back I hurried up West Hill*
> *To catch you on your morning walk to school,*

His poems record visits made to Berkshire in these early years; 'Indoor Games near

Newbury' recreates 'Wendy's party' with 'lemon curd and Christmas cake' and the drive through the countryside to reach her house:

> *In among the silver birches winding ways of tarmac wander*
> *And the signs to Bussock Bottom, Tussock Wood and Windy Brake,*
> *Gabled lodges, tile hung churches, catch the lights of our Lagonda,*

Bussock Camp Fort can certainly be found to the north-west of Newbury, as can Bussock Wood, Bussock Mayne and Bussock Hill House. Evocative names that rhyme often feature in Betjeman's poetry and, as here, some poetic licence adds to the fun. Living at the time and in the way that they did, the Betjeman family had no need to walk, but many references to footpaths and stiles in the poems show that strolling in the country was a frequent pleasure. In 'Norfolk' the poet remembers a boyhood holiday he once had:

> *The years fall off and find me walking back...*
> *Down this same path, where, forty years ago,*
> *My father strolled behind me, calm and slow.*
>
> *I used to fill my hands with sorrel seeds*
> *And shower him with them from the tops of stiles*
> *I used to butt my head into his tweeds*
> *To make him hurry down those languorous miles*
> *Of ash and alder-shaded lanes...*

Life was not all holidays. At Highgate Junior School there were bullies, but one master, TS Eliot, was clearly trusted; he was presented with a manuscript, 'The Best of Betjeman' – a hint at the future, whatever the quality of the writing. When he was eleven, John was sent as a boarder to the Dragon School in Oxford; an untypical pupil, he carried a book of poetry in his pocket, won speaking competitions and excelled at acting. Free time was spent cycling deep into the countryside with a like-minded friend or teacher to visit churches or search for wild flowers. He was less happy at Marlborough School but enjoyed sketching expeditions when, with pencil and watercolour, the boys would try to capture the shape of a thatched barn, a clump of trees or changes in light. Betjeman's interest in landscape and well-crafted buildings developed during his university years in Oxford and expanded further as his writing and publishing activities grew.

Walkers tend to share Betjeman's appreciation of a world just past; his writings and talks urged conservation before it was a universal plea and 'time redeemed', not just 'time remembered', is a key theme. The sardonic tone of 'The Dear Old Village', where three bells are rung instead of six because of a 'row about the ringers' tea' is far more persuasive than a lecture. Although some of the incidents Betjeman mentions – for example, 'Farmers have wired the public rights-of-way / Should any wish to walk to church to pray' – are, unfortunately, still familiar, many landowners nowadays are a far cry from Farmer Whistle:

> He takes no part in village life beyond
> Throwing his refuse in a neighbour's pond
> And closing foot paths, not repairing walls
> Leaving a cottage till at last it falls.
> People protest. A law-suit then begins,
> But as he's on the Bench, he always wins.

So, Betjeman, in the 1950s, with his humorous, rhyming verse, opened eyes to the loss of public rights and heritage. Nowadays, taking action to preserve the country they explore and the paths they walk on has become an accepted duty for many ramblers.

In July 1933 Betjeman married Penelope Chetwode; she was a clever, lively woman, with her own interests and a love of foreign travel. He hated the idea of travel abroad but she shared many of his delights. In a note written in June of that year she wrote: 'I love the English country so much and seeing it with you is a revelation'. Penelope had lived in India, where her father was Commander-in-Chief of the army, and had enjoyed studying India's temples and culture. She was also a keen horsewoman.

John Betjeman and Penelope first came to Berkshire to live in 1934. He worked mainly in London but they both preferred the calm of the country. A farmhouse, at the modest rent of £36 a year, was found for them in the village of Uffington, in the Vale of the White Horse, which was then in Berkshire. Garrard's Farm suited them well, as did the church – Early English with an imposing tower – where Betjeman became churchwarden. There were the downs and the Ridgeway, where Penelope rode on her Arab mare, Moti. She also kept a goat, Snowdrop, that gave milk. The Great Western Railway trains, from nearby Challow Station, took Betjeman to work and brought friends to visit; Evelyn Waugh, Osbert Lancaster and other well-known people stayed with them. They made friends locally too, and often went to dinner with Lord Berners of Farringdon Hall. He was a composer admired by Stravinsky and he painted Penelope, with Moti, in the hall of his Georgian mansion. The Betjemans also enjoyed taking part in village life; a comic drawing by Lancaster shows them in full voice in the Uffington concert of 1935. As churchwarden, Betjeman supervised the conversion of the gas lighting to electricity, paid for the cleaning of the royal arms and revived the holding of Mummers plays in the village.

In 1938 the family's first child, Paul, was born; he was put on a horse before he could walk and into a toy train soon after by his fond father. Life must have been busy and jolly at Garrard's Farm, though the only poem to refer directly to the village is sombre. In 'Uffington' he speaks of the 'muffled peal' of the church bells, which have a 'death-reminding dying fall' that makes 'Even the trivial seems profound'.

Between 1934 and 1941 Betjeman co-edited with John Piper the *Shell Guides* to the counties of England. He also published his volumes of poetry *Continual Dew* and *Old Lights for New Chancels*. War service as a Press Attaché in Dublin intervened and daughter Candida was born there in 1942. The Betjeman family came back to Berkshire in 1945.

JOHN BETJEMAN

Penelope wrote to a friend, Wilhelmine Harrod, in July of that year;

> Father has bought us a beautiful William and Mary house 700 feet up on the downs above Wantage, with 12 acres of land, including a wood and two fields. It is a dream of beauty but has no water and no light and is falling down and needs six servants, so it will probably kill us in the end.

The Old Rectory in the village of Farnborough is a beautiful house. It stands opposite All Saints Church, which is partly Norman; a fine window can be seen inside, with the inscription:

In memory of John Betjeman, 1906–1984. Poet Laureate, sometime resident at The Old Rectory, Farnborough. This window designed by his friend, John Piper, and executed by Joseph Nuttgens, placed here by the Friends of Friendless Churches. I am the Resurrection and the Life.

From Farnborough, as from Uffington, footpaths lead in many directions and the prehistoric Ridgeway is even nearer. The downs, where horses are trained on the wide stretches of the gallops, the tree-lined river valleys, where lives have been spent in service, is the subject matter of 'Upper Lamborne'; it evokes a part of Berkshire well loved for walking.

The Old Rectory, Farnborough.

Feathery ash in leathery Lambourne
Waves above the sarsen stone,
And Edwardian plantations
So coniferously moan
As to make the swelling downland,
Far-surrounding, seem their own.

Betjeman's achievements during the years in Farnborough were many; his collection of verse *New Bats in Old Belfries* was published in 1945, and in 1948 his *Selected Poems*, edited by John Sparrow, won the Heinemann Award for Literature. The co-editing with John Piper continued; in 1949 Murray's *Architectural Guide for Berkshire* was published.

In 1951 the Betjemans found a third home in Berkshire. They moved to a dignified, Victorian brick-built house in Wantage, called The Mead, with stables and a tennis court in its spacious gardens. Betjeman often worked in his London flat during the week, but he would return home by train to hear 'the bells through the apple bloom – Sunday-ly sounding'. Wantage was in Berkshire until the 1974 boundary changes, as was all the Vale of the White Horse, and proud of its history. King Alfred's statue stands in Wantage Square and The Mead is thought to be on the site of the palace where he was born; it certainly stands alongside the the Anglo-Saxon Icknield Way.

Moving to Wantage gave Penelope Betjeman the opportunity to establish an enterprise or two of her own; she set up The Mead Waterfowl Farm, where she bred ducks and geese, and a tea-shop called King Alfred's Kitchen. She continued to explore the downs on horseback and, in later years, her daughter Candida placed a sarsen stone on the Ridgeway in her memory.

During the years in Wantage, John Betjeman's appearances on television, in programmes like the Brains Trust, became more frequent; collections such as *A Few Late Chrysanthemums* and *High and Low*, which contain some of his best poetry, were published, as was his blank verse autobiography, *Summoned by Bells*. Honours came too; the CBE in 1960, a knighthood in 1969 and Poet Laureate in 1972. From this time, John Betjeman and his wife began to live apart, though they remained good friends. In *On Leaving Wantage* (1972) he records his feelings:

I like the way these old brick garden walls
Unevenly run down to Letcombe Brook.
I like the mist of green about the elms
In earliest leaf time.

The last section of the poem suggests regret and some confusion:

From this wide vale, where all our married lives
We two have lived, we now are whirled away

JOHN BETJEMAN – WALK 15

Momently clinging to the things we knew –
Friends, footpaths, hedges, house and animals
Till, borne along like twigs and bits of straw,
We sink below the sliding stream of time.

In a television interview in 1984, the year of his death, Betjeman said 'poetry makes life worth living'. He added that the most valuable thing he had done was to use his eyes and his feelings. When we walk 'by stile and footbridge', as he so often did in his 'spontaneous Berkshire days', we can reflect that one of his many achievements was to help to keep the footpaths open so we too can enjoy the countryside he described so well.

WALK 15

A JOHN BETJEMAN WALK OF SIX OR SEVEN MILES FROM FARNBOROUGH IN BERKSHIRE

Ordnance Survey Landranger Sheet 174
START POINT: grid reference 436819

from 1945 to 1951; at the time of writing, the gardens of the Old Vicarage are open to the public several times a year in aid of the National Gardens Scheme. Walk forward, and, as the road bends left, follow a signed footpath on the right. Ahead, at more signs, choose the footpath, not the bridleway, and walk across the field ahead and slightly left. In summer there may be rape growing here; in full flower, it will be thick with bees and butterflies.

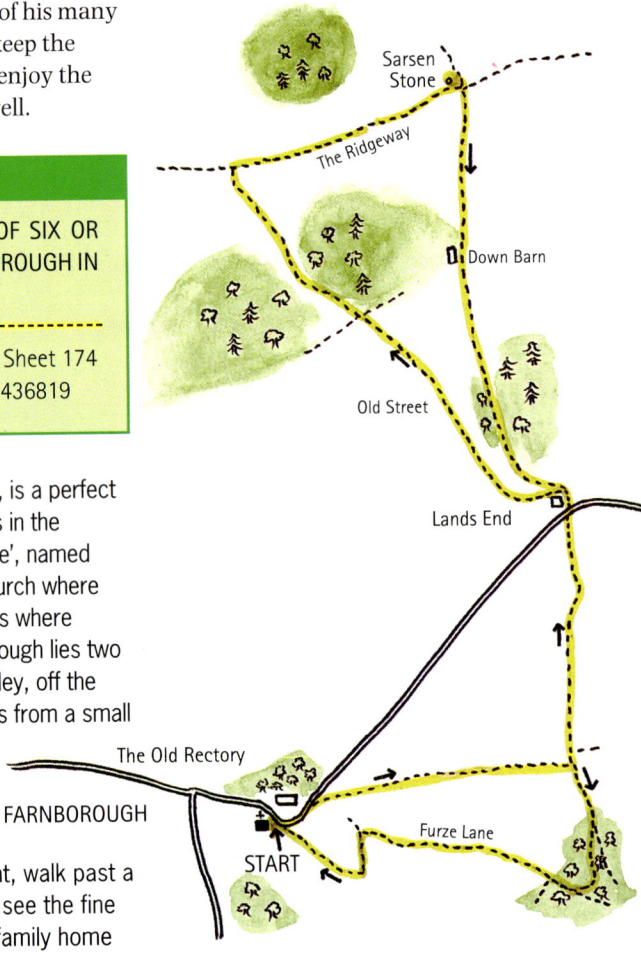

FARNBOROUGH, IN BERKSHIRE, is a perfect place to ramble. This walk takes in the 'beautiful William and Mary house', named The Old Vicarage, All Saints' Church where Betjeman served, and the downs where Penelope loved to ride. Farnborough lies two and a half miles west of East Ilsley, off the A34 trunk road. The walk begins from a small parking area near All Saints Church. It is six miles long, or seven if you take the extended route at **.

With the church on your right, walk past a telephone box and look left to see the fine house that was the Betjeman family home

98

At the first hedge and signs, cross the next field slightly right, to reach a wide path and signpost. Turn left into this path, which is Old Street, a trackway as old as the Ridgeway. Follow it downhill, ignoring side paths, to reach a road which you cross; walk a few yards to the right and take a track on the left, which passes to the right of the house called Lands End. Behind the house take the grassy path on the left, still Old Street, and walk up through a beautiful valley where wild blue geranium, willowherb and green woodpeckers can be spotted in summer.

Ignore a farm track crossing the path; keep ahead, for over a mile, until you come to the Ridgeway. Here there are fine views, sweeping down towards Wantage and far into Oxfordshire. Turn right and walk for about half a mile, to where footpath signs show that another track crosses the Ridgeway. Here, if you look carefully, you can find a sarsen stone, dedicated to Penelope Betjeman by her daughter Candida to commemorate her love of this ancient track. To find the stone, walk off the Ridgeway a few yards, as if you were going to follow the left-hand path, then turn and look back. The memorial is under a hawthorn tree on the right.

Return to the Ridgeway and take the path that leaves it on the opposite side; walk down a broad gravel track, passing a farm, to reach Lands End house again. Cross the road and walk back up Old Street to the point at which you joined it on the outward route.
** Here you can either return the way you came or extend the walk by about a mile.

For the latter, continue ahead until you reach a marker post on the right; here turn off the main track along a woodland path to the right, bright with bluebells in spring. Keep right when a path joins from the left and, at the next footpath signs, ignore the byway on the left, continue ahead for half a mile on an old track, Furze Lane. At more signs, turn left on a bridleway, with a hedge on your right, and soon turn right along a field edge to reach a stile in the right corner of the field; cross this into another field. By now All Saint's Church should be visible ahead; this is reached by crossing two small fields with stiles. If you have not already done so, finish your 'pilgrimage' by visiting the church, to enjoy its quiet peace and to see the window designed by John Piper in memory of his friend.

Garrard's Farm, Uffington, and The Mead, in Wantage, can both be found.

Uffington lies seven miles west of Wantage and can be reached by taking a turning off the B4507. Garrard's Farm, opposite the Fox and Hounds, is a long low house, in a quiet rural setting below the downs, where the White Horse has been groomed through the centuries. Still presiding, on the north side of the village, is St Mary's Church; John Betjeman was a churchwarden while he lived in the village. The Thomas Hughes walk, Walk 5, passes both the church and Garrard's Farm.

To find The Mead, leave Market Square in Wantage, in the direction that King Alfred is facing, pass the Church of St Peter and St Paul, and walk down Priory Road. Turn right into Locks Lane, find and cross the bridge over a small stream and walk left along a path, with the house above on your right. You will come to the gates at the entrance of the drive to The Mead, a solid Victorian house with rambling outbuildings. Penelope Betjeman's teashop, King Alfred's Kitchen, is now the Peking Dynasty; it still juts out into the street, although protests were made that it was a hazard to traffic even when the Betjemans rented it.

MORE WRITERS OF TOWN AND COUNTRY

A SHORT RECORD is made in this section of a number of writers who lived only briefly in Berkshire but nevertheless recorded experiences in its towns and countryside.

PERCY BYSSHE SHELLEY, 1792–1822, lived for just a short time in both Windsor and Bracknell. He was born into a wealthy, worldly family with scant tolerance of his radical, amoral views and poetic aspiration. As a result, he was kept very short of money. Moving often, to escape creditors or others upset by his behaviour, Shelley and his wife Harriet came first to High Elms, in Bracknell, in July 1813. Reeds Hill Farm, near Church Hill House Hospital, in Crowthorne Road, is also thought to have been rented by Shelley. The sonnet 'Evening: to Harriet', written then, speaks of the sun sinking 'over cobweb lawn and grove and stream'; no gazer could then find fault with earth's beauty. The poem concludes:

> Such were thy lover, Harriet, could he fly
> The thoughts of all that makes his passion dear,
> And, turning senseless from thy warm caress,
> Pick flaws in our close-woven happiness.

The romance soon lost its bloom; in 'At Bracknell', written in 1814, 'the lover' writes:

> Thy dewy looks sink in my breast;
> Thy gentle words stir poison there;
> Thou has disturbed the only rest
> That was the portion of despair!

Harriet, with her baby daughter Ianthe and her sister Eliza, left the house at Windsor they had taken for a short while. Shelley also had kept rooms with Mrs de Boinville and her daughter in Bracknell, but he was asked to move from these now he was a 'grass widower'. In 'Stanzas, April 1814' he regrets he must return to a 'sad and silent' Windsor home and leave the Boinvilles and 'that house and heath and garden' made dear to him by 'the music of two voices and the light of one sweet smile'.

As his poetry shows, Shelley was inspired by nature's beauty and was restored to serenity by walking in the countryside. In August 1815 he embarked on a river trip, which improved his physical health and also provided ideas and images for 'Alastor', one of his finest poems. He set out with Mary Wollstonecraft Godwin, who was to become his second wife, with the poet Thomas Love Peacock and another friend Charles Clairmont, to discover the source of the Thames. The river described by the poet hero in 'Alastor' recalls the rocky mountain streams that

Shelley had seen on wider travels but also, very clearly, the Thames:

> ...Now on the polished stones
> It danced; like childhood laughing as it went;
> Then through the plain in tranquil wanderings crept
> Reflecting every herb and drooping bud
> That overhung its quietness.

Mary Shelley later wrote *Frankenstein* and, after her husband's death from drowning in Italy, returned to England and wrote novels and travel books. Her journal records visits to Berkshire.

Thomas Love Peacock, at whose home in Marlow Shelley often lived, used his knowledge of the river in his long poem 'The Genius of The Thames'; in this he speaks of its calm beauty and its place in England's history.

HERBERT GEORGE WELLS, 1866–1946, lived in Berkshire in his youth and later used his memories of the Thames in his novels. He was apprenticed in Windsor to the drapers Rogers and Denyer; a plaque in the High Street, near Token House, shows where the shop stood. His training is featured in his novel *Mr Kipps*. He did not suit his employers for long, though, and he returned to Uppark, Sussex, where his mother was housekeeper, finding its library a more congenial place to spend his time.

Much of his life was spent in London, but Wells often escaped to the country. As a boy he spent his summer holidays with Uncle Tom, who kept Surly Inn, on the Thames near Windsor. His autobiography records his taking Ellen Terry and Henry Irving on the river in a punt. Such events later gave him material for *The History of Mr Polly*, whose hero leaves a mundane marriage to become odd-job-man for a plump, pleasant landlady at the Potwell Inn. Wells would also have drawn inspiration from The Beetle and Wedge, Moulsford, near Streatley, where he stayed while he was writing. Mr Polly, with punt pole, rampages on the river bank, putting an end to Uncle Jim's bullying ways. He cries 'You keep out' – and so the Potwell Inn is restored to gentle peace. The story, full of rollicking fun, became one of Wells's most popular.

Walking features in some of Wells's novels and in accounts of his life. In *Kipps* the hero tells the heroine as they cross a field with a bull in it, 'walk quietly towards the stile', and he shouts at the aggressive animal, 'You be off'. Wells enjoyed taking exercise near his home in Castle Eaton with guests, but overweight GK Chesterton protested: 'We don't go for a walk to-day do we?' Wells stayed in Berkshire on another occasion: although he had left his first wife, Isabel, early in their marriage, he did not forget her and one summer day he decided to cycle to Twyford to see her. The two spent the day near Virginia Water and he stayed the night at her poultry farm. Next day he cycled off again, but he kept his concern for her; he and his second wife, Catherine, later nursed her through illness and had her living with them. When she was fit again, she joined Wells in long country walks.

ROBERT GIBBINGS, 1889–1958, wrote in his preface to *Sweet Thames Run Softly* that as he had travelled 'fifty thousand miles over salt water', it now 'might be fun to explore the River Thames in whose valley' he had lived by then for fifteen

101

years. Already an established writer of books on wildlife and travel, he built a flat-bottomed boat, helped by his son and friends at Reading University, where he was a lecturer. The boat, to be propelled by sculls, was completed in a fortnight and it never took in 'as much as a bead of water'.

Always a strong walker, Gibbings covered the twenty-two miles from the source of the Thames to Lechlade on foot, then boarded his boat to continue his voyage downstream. From Buscot to below Windsor, the Thames formed the northern boundary of Berkshire at that time, and the Gibbings family were living a little to the south of the river, in Footbridge Cottage, Long Wittenham. Both text and drawings that record this journey reveal a close knowledge of wildlife, as can be seen from this description of early morning on the river:

The banks glided back; no sound, no jar. As dawn crept in, colour began to show, and I could make out the markings of some cattle on the bank. Only a few moments earlier these same creatures had been no more than silhouettes. It reminded me of polishing stone or timber – the way the grain of the landscape came up, willows and an occasional elm, grey against the sky, clumps of yellow loosestrife and willow-herb standing out from the pale comfrey that lined the banks.

As he glides past, he also pictures wider views, such as the Berkshire Downs, west from the Goring Gap, 'some of the grandest scenery on the river'; behind 'a fringe of luxuriant chestnuts, maple trees and acacias, hills rise steeply, dotted with chalk pits and crested with beechwoods'. Gibbings's own fine etchings of birds, plant-life and landscape illustrate his words; in 1926 he had bought the Golden Cockerel Press, located at Waltham St Lawrence, and designed books and engravings there. The titles of two of these books are taken from *Prothalamion*, written by Edmund Spenser in 1596 to honour a betrothal; each stanza ends with: 'Sweete Themmes! runne softly, till I end my Song.'

'We should learn to walk slowly, so that we have time to see,' Robert Gibbings advises those who explore the countryside, 'tracks in winter snow, flights of summer butterflies or actions of nesting birds will all then add new interest and understanding.'

The Thames National Footpath, from the source to Reading, which is well signposted and described in a number of guides, would be a route worth following with Robert Gibbings's *Sweet Thames Run Softly* in your pocket.

MISS READ (DORA SAINT), 1913–, gives an appealing picture of village life. Miss Read and Mrs Saint's other characters, their daily lives and their memories, are drawn from years of experience living in Shefford Woodlands, a hamlet a few miles north-east of Hungerford, in Berkshire. But they are typical of villages everywhere, and this accounts for Miss Read's popularity.

By no means all aspects of life are comfortable:

> *This lane leads to the downs, which shelter our village from the north-east wind...the road narrows, tarmac finishes and only a muddy track makes its way uphill to peter out...on the windy slopes high above.*

But summer brings changes: 'in shimmering heat, small blue butterflies of the chalk downs hover in still air. Miss Read pauses by a field gate on her way to visit a teacher colleague and admires the view:

> *Scarlet poppies dropped a petal or two and high in the blue, a hawk hovered motionless for a while and then painted invisible circles with its wing-tip, slipping languidly and elegantly round the sky.*

Mrs Saint does not often show her villagers out walking – some even puff as they climb the hills – but taking paths across fields to church or to school is so much a part of country life that it goes without saying!

In April 1998 *The Times* reported that 'Miss Read' had reached her eighty-fifth birthday; perhaps it is the open air of the downs that has helped her pass this milestone.

RICHARD ADAMS, 1920–, spent his early life in Wash Common, to the south-west of Newbury. An absorbing account of this part of the county in the 1920s is given in his autobiography *The Day Gone By*, published in 1990. His doctor father bought a practice in Newbury when his own father died, and moved his family to a 'beautiful house out at Wash Common', where Richard was born in 1920. 'It certainly was a splendid place to grow up,' says Adams. Oakdene, built in 1895, was large, with seven bedrooms, three acres of land, a gardener's cottage, paddock, orchard, 'wild wood' and much more. The writer adds: 'The superb view to the south was across the open country of ploughland, meadows and copses typical of the Berkshire–Hampshire border.'

Adams describes being fascinated by wildlife and his father taught him to love the birds that came in large numbers to the 'half-wild, wooded and lawned garden'. He also took him to paddle in the Enborne, a stream that forms the boundary between Berkshire and Hampshire:

> *This was the first stream I ever knew. It was, and still is, as pretty a brook as could be imagined, in places roofed over with alder in summer, all the air heavy with the scent of meadowsweet, the shallows full of blue brooklime. I remember big, green dragonflies hovering and darting over the water.*

The two often walked on Greenham Common, where the young boy once saw a stoat and watched a spider spinning a web in the bracken. Adams was clearly a good walker also; at eight years old, having quarrelled with his older sister, he set out to 'go away and be alone'. He walked across Greenham to Brimpton, about seven miles, and then decided he had better return; he was so tired he despaired of reaching home but luckily a bigger boy on a bicycle gave him a lift. A favourite place for exploring was the Wilderness, found halfway between Newbury and Hungerford, down a lane with 'hedges covered with honeysuckle and dog rose'; it took father and son to the 'broad Kennet spanned by a plank footbridge'. 'Almost the first thing I saw', writes Adams, 'was a kingfisher flying past us fast and low on the other side of the river.'

Richard Adams was sent to Horris Hill School, then to Bradfield College, where he particularly enjoyed taking part in Greek and Shakespeare plays performed in the open-air theatre. He worked hard and won a scholarship to Worcester College, Oxford; the Second World War intervened, though, so his university studies were deferred until it was over.

His father's health and his medical practice were failing, so Oakdene was sold in 1939, and the family moved into the gardener's cottage. The big house no longer exists and Newbury has now engulfed Wash Common.

After the war, Adams returned to Oxford, gained his degree, then joined the Civil Service in the Department of the Environment. As a boy, he had written poetry and told stories, and later he wrote articles, often expressing firm views; in *The Day Gone By* he says: 'Why can't Greenham Common now be restored as a public open space.' In the early 1960s he was planning a major novel. By then Adams was married to Elizabeth and had two daughters, Juliet and Rosamund; to pass the time on a long car journey, he told them stories about the rabbits he had watched as a boy. The novel is based on his detailed observation of local wildlife and his knowledge of plants and the weather: the warren where Hazel, Fiver, Bigwig and the other rabbits began life was on Sandleford Common, just in front of Oakdene; the River Enborne, which the rabbits had to cross to make their escape, could be seen from the windows of the house, and Watership Down was visible on the horizon. Fiver's sixth sense tells him that danger is coming to the Sandleford Warren and the reader is told that Sutch and Martin, of Newbury, Berks, are going to build houses there, so clearly the rabbits will be destroyed. Thus Adams brings together aspects of his early days and his later employment. With his knowledge of country life, he gives his rabbits believable reactions and creates tension as they face danger. Here Hazel is escaping:

From the moment he entered it, the wood seemed full of noises. There was a smell of damp leaves and moss and everywhere the splash of water went whispering about. Just inside, the brook made a little fall into a pool and the sound enclosed among the trees, echoed as if in a cave. Roosting birds rustled overhead; the night breeze stirred the leaves; here and there a dead twig fell.

Watership Down is Richard Adams's best-known book. At least six hardback editions have been printed and thousands of paperbacks sell each day. It won the Carnegie Medal and a Guardian Award for Children's Fiction. Adams was able to retire in 1974 and devote all his time to writing a fine range of novels, nature and travel books. In recent years he has lived in Streatley, so he has not lost touch with the county in which he grew up.

VISITING WRITERS TO RIDGEWAY AND RIVER

BERKSHIRE'S ANCIENT TRACKWAYS and historic rivers have added magic to some of the finest English literature. Writers in this section, though not resident in Berkshire, have made the county unforgettable to generations of readers. The parts of the Thames that many of them loved can be seen by walking on the Thames Path, which is shown on Ordnance Survey Landranger Sheets 174 and 175.

WALTER SCOTT, 1771–1832, in his historical novel *Kenilworth*, uses a number of locations that suggest he knew the Berkshire of his day well. Cumnor Place, the main setting for the tragedy, is first introduced by ballad, then mention is made of other corners of the county, such as Yattendon and Donnington Castle, while names like Micheal Lambourne, Prance of Padworth and Old Thatcham, hint further at the location. *Kenilworth*, though, is a novel born of books, based in history, even if it is adapted to give form. 'If we can trust Ashmole's *Antiquities of Berkshire*,' Scott says, 'there was but too much ground for the traditions which charge Leicester with the murder of his wife.' He also had help to glean the necessary facts; a letter in 1820 asks:

> What was the name of Dudley, Earl of Leicester's, first wife, whom he was supposed to have murdered at Cumnor Hall, in Berkshire?...in Lyson's *Magna Britannia*...there is something about this same Cumnor Hall. I wish you would have it copied out for me and I should like to know anything that occurs to you about the village of Cumnor, its situation, etc. I like to be as minutely local as I can.

Wayland Smithy, the impressive ancient burial monument on the Ridgeway near Ashbury, gives Scott more material; Wayland, or Weland in early Anglo-Saxon legend and poetry, a smith of great skill, is linked with the stone burial chamber. In *Kenilworth* Wayland becomes a character living near the smithy in an underground cell, from which he emerges to shoe horses, as in the legends, but where he also prepares the antidotes to poisons that are threatening the heroine's life.

Walter Scott could have visited Berkshire; Thomas Hughes's grandmother certainly stayed with him in Edinburgh, and his son was tutored, for a time, in Uffington Rectory; whether he did or not visit, acquaintance with his stories adds colour to walks in Lambourn Downs country.

ALFRED TENNYSON, 1809–1892, adopted Berkshire identity from the family background of his wife, who was born Emily Sellwood. He often travelled through the county, and his marriage took place in Shiplake Church, just across the Thames. Tennyson first met Emily in 1829, when their families became acquainted; she then lived in Horncastle, near to the Tennyson's Lincolnshire home, Somersby, but came of a landed Berkshire family who had by then lost their money. Friendship developed during long walks in nearby Holywell Wood; an engagement in 1836 was broken but rifts were at last healed with the help of friends and relatives, and the marriage took place in 1850. The first night of the honeymoon was spent in Pangbourne, on the Berkshire side of the Thames!

In 1865 Tennyson, now with an acclaimed reputation and a sound income, bought land on the Sussex Weald, facing the sea, and built a house, which was called Aldworth after the Berkshire village that had formed part of the estate of Emily's forebears. 'It wants nothing but a great river looping along through the midst of it,' the poet said, no doubt thinking of the Thames. The Thames was probably the model for lines like 'On either side the river lie / Long fields of barley and of rye', with which *The Lady of Shallott* begins. When, in 1883, Tennyson was honoured with a peerage, he chose Baron Tennyson of Aldworth and Freshwater as his title.

MATTHEW ARNOLD, 1822–1888, was also strongly influenced by the Thames. It links themes in much of his finest poetry and formed a background for many important times in his life. He was born on Christmas Eve 1822 in the village of Laleham, by the Thames, and grew up in a respected and cultured family. He left Rugby School – where his father, Dr Thomas Arnold, had as headmaster improved the educational experience of pupils – and having won a scholarship to Balliol College, Oxford, came back to live near the Thames again.

The most notable friendship of these school and college years was with Arthur Hugh Clough; both young men had written poetry at school and began publishing soon after gaining their degrees. The Thames and nearby countryside formed the settings for much of their writing. They were energetic and enjoyed the open air; they would skiff upriver to Bablock Hythe, or walk south into Berkshire to Cumnor and beyond. In *The Scholar-Gipsy*, Arnold shows students trying to trace their poor friend who, 'tired of knocking on preferment's door', abandoned his college studies and 'went to learn the gipsy-lore'. They learned that shepherds had seen him 'At some lone alehouse in the Berkshire moors'. The poet, himself, lies in his boat:

Moored to the cool bank in the summer-heats
'Mid wide grass meadows which the sunshine fills,

Later he sees some who have spent the day in the country returning home, 'Crossing the stripling Thames at Bab-lock-Hithe'. Arnold's apt phrase for the river west of Oxford, 'the stripling Thames', has been used by many later writers.

Clough died in Italy in 1861; his widow sent some of his last poems to Arnold who told her, 'I shall take them with me to Oxford, where I shall go alone after Easter and there, among the Cumnor hills where we have so often rambled, I shall be able to think him over as I wish.' His moving elegy for Clough, 'Thyrsis', was inspired by this visit. He asks,

Runs it not here, the track by Childsworth Farm,
Past the high wood to where the elm tree crowns
The hill behind whose ridge the sunset flames?

The poem revisits all the places of significance to them and recalls their beauty at differing seasons of the year. That signal-elm, their special symbol, is gone; the mowers, too, who 'stood with scythes suspended' to see them pass. 'They are all gone, and thou are gone as well!'

Matthew Arnold journied widely, finding wild plants of special interest; writing about a drive out to the Berkshire Hills of Massachusetts, USA, he mentions 'great meadow rue, beautifully elegant, the *Helianthus giganteus* and milkweed' and many other plants. He was, however, most at ease in places that were familiar. When he died in 1888, he was buried in Laleham churchyard, at rest with other members of his family and close, once more, to the Thames.

WILLIAM MORRIS, 1834–1896, also seemed at his happiest in Thames country. He joined friends for boating trips up the 'lonely far-off mother of the Thames' while he was at Oxford, and Kelmscott Manor, which he bought in 1871, 'gave him twenty-five years of exquisite peace'. In *News From Nowhere*, a journey upriver ends at Kelmscott; the narrator is transposed into the year 2003, when a return to crafts and farming methods that had been practised before the industrial era is seen to have brought a simple but contented life. Kelmscott Manor fits well its Thames-side setting; it is two miles east of Lechlade and is open to the public. Aspects of Morris's philosophy, as well as fine examples of his craftwork, are to be discovered there.

RUDYARD KIPLING, 1868–1932, wrote of historical events linked with the Thames and also refers to Berkshire history and legend, though he did not live in the county. In *Puck of Pook's Hill* he involves Wayland-Smith in a web of archaeology, history and myth. Like Scott, he adapts legend for his own purpose. We meet Weland on the chalk hills of the Sussex Downs, where Kipling built his family home, Bateman's; the sprite Puck tells of the 'smith of the gods' shoeing horses and forging magical swords – but he also speaks of having met him on inland downs earlier. In the same book Puck tells of 'the Law that was signed at Runnymede' and of 'Magna Charta' signed on the island in the Thames that carries its name. In the last verse of *The Reeds of Runnymede* Kipling develops these ideas:

> And still when Mob or Monarch lays
> Too rude a hand on English ways
> And whisper wakes, the shudder plays,
> Across the reeds at Runnymede.
> And Thames, that knows the moods of kings,
> And crowds and priests and suchlike things
> Rolls deep and dreadful as he brings
> Their warning down from Runnymede!

GEORGE ORWELL, 1903–1950, spent his early days across the Thames from Berkshire in Henley and Shiplake. He was at Eton College and later, after years abroad and living in cities, returned to the countryside. He lived with the Warburg family at Scarlett's Farm, in 'lush meadows', near Twyford, Berkshire; *The Lion and the Unicorn* was written while Second World War bombers flew overhead. He loved outdoor pursuits and often took long walks. In *Keep the Aspidistra Flying*, the most autobiographical of Orwell's novels,

Gordon Comstock takes his girl, Rosemary, for a walk in the countryside. When, in 1945, Orwell spent Christmas with writer friend, Arthur Koestler, the two of them 'went for a long country walk, Orwell carrying his adopted son, Richard, Asian-style on his hip'.

George Orwell died in January 1950; a simple stone marks his grave in All Saints churchyard, Sutton Courtney, south of Abingdon, which was then in Berkshire.

THOMAS HARDY, 1840–1928, in his preface to *Jude the Obscure*, wrote 'The scenes were revisited in October, 1892'. Much of this novel is set in Berkshire, or North Wessex as Hardy called it; although he did not live in this county he knew its landscape, villages and towns quite well. Despite this, he rewalked those areas that would suit the plan of his novel, creating a picture of the county that rang true at that time and in some ways has not changed much since.

Hardy uses fictitious names, but gives such precise detail that locations are easy to identify. Jude leaves the cottage in Marygreen [Fawley on a map], which he shares with his aunt, and walks a public footpath, a 'white road' that 'seemed to ascend till it reached the sky', where 'it was crossed, at right angles, by a green ridgeway'. Jude dreamed of studying in Christminster, [or Oxford], which was about fifteen miles to the north-east, so he waited until the mist lifted just before sunset, then climbed a ladder, left by workmen at the Brown [Red] House, and saw its 'vanes, windows, wet roof slates and other shining spots upon the spires. It was Christminster unquestionably.' Later, from the same place on the Ridgeway, Jude and Arabella 'looking over the vast northern landscape' saw a fire at Alfredston [or Wantage] and ran three miles down into the town to look. In Cresscombe [Letcombe Bassett], to the Ridgeway's north, there is a house called 'Arabella's Cottage'; even if it does not quite fit Hardy's details of her 'small homestead', it lies on a route Jude could have taken to his work in Alfredston. Aldbrickham [Reading] and Kennetbridge [Newbury] are also the settings for later chapters of the novel. Sue and Jude stayed at The George Hotel in King Street, Reading, as well as in Spring Street, then 'a lane almost out in the country', perhaps near Spring Gardens, which still exist. Arabella came to Kennetbridge to see foundations set for a new Baptist chapel; this stood in the town centre until a new one was built at St Mary's Hill.

In other stories, too, there are Berkshire locations. 'Castle Royal' is Windsor Castle, and a lady from Sulhamstead claimed that the writer said he had put her village into his short story *The Son's Veto*, giving it the name Gaymead.

VISITING WRITERS TO RIDGEWAY AND RIVER – WALK 16

Arabella's Cottage

WALK 16

A FIVE-MILE WALK IN THOMAS HARDY'S NORTH WESSEX, WHICH ALSO PASSES WHERE DEAN SWIFT STAYED IN 1714

Ordnance Survey Landranger Sheet 174
START POINT: grid reference 393853

THE RIDGEWAY, ANCIENT and spectacular, has featured so frequently in literature that perhaps more people have walked it in their mind's eye than in reality. And many of the villages lying below the down have almost as long a history. This five-mile walk, from the high slopes of the downs south of Wantage down to Letcombe Bassett and back, traces some of the routes Hardy would have taken as he planned the course of Jude's actions. It also passes the Old Rectory, where Johnathan Swift stayed in 1714.

The walk starts at the Courthill Ridgeway Centre, found by turning off the A338 about two miles south of Wantage, on to the Letcombe Regis road. The Centre is on the left and can, at the time of writing, be reached by the Ridgeway Explorer Bus. Park in a lay-by just before the Centre's gate.

109

VISITING WRITERS TO RIDGEWAY AND RIVER – WALK 16

Turn left from the Centre and walk down the road for about half a mile, with a wide view of the countryside towards Wantage before you. Turn left into a fenced track and left again at a small road to pass houses. Just past Warborough Farm, cross a stile on the right with a Countryside Commission sign and walk ahead through fields, keeping near to a fence on the right and crossing stiles at field boundaries.

At a path junction, ignore the small noticeboard, but take a stile on the right, then one on the left. Cross a field diagonally left to find a stile and a path through trees. Take this path and, as the trees end, cross a stile and, ignoring a signpost left at this point, turn right, cross a stile, then turn left and, keeping a fence on your left, reach another stile to a lane.

Turn right and walk down towards Letcombe Bassett. The white house on first right, double-fronted with a wide courtyard, is the Old Rectory. This is where Dr Dean Swift was staying in 1714, when Alexander Pope and Thomas Parnell rode thirty miles, through rain, to visit him. Swift, who paid his host, Reverend John Geree, a guinea a week, spent time here reading and walking. The Vicar of Wantage rode to the isolated village to tell him of the death of Queen Anne; the 'Vanessa' of his poems also visited, though he chided her for indiscretion, in a later letter.

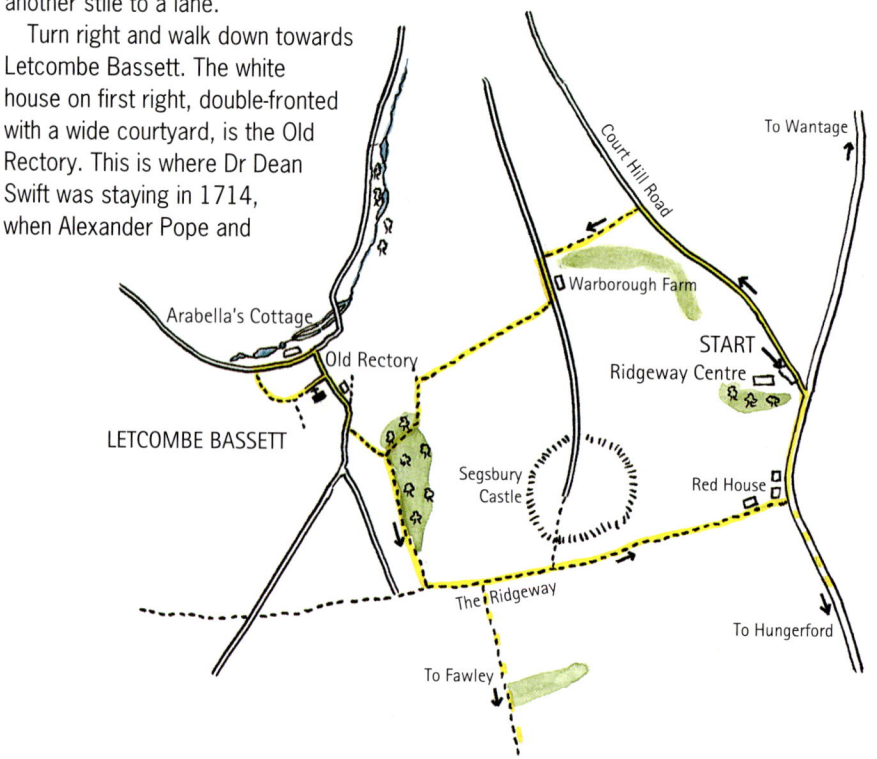

Continue downhill, ignoring a no-through road on the left, to a T-junction with road signs; here turn left and, on the right-hand side of the road, after the old Chapel and Chapel Cottage, find Arabella's Cottage. In one or two ways it does not fit Hardy's description in the novel; he writes, 'on the further side of the stream stood a small homestead' with garden and pigsties. The stream in fact runs behind the delightfully kept house in its pleasant garden, but writers make adaptations and this cottage, which was no doubt smaller when Hardy found it, must have seemed a suitable place for Jude's first encounter with Arabella and her giggling friends. Intent on his future study plans, Jude had chosen a quieter, though longer, walk to work in Alfredston, as he explains to Arabella when he asks her name: 'I must have known it if I had often come this way. But I mostly go straight along the high-road.' Letcombe Bassett, named Cresscombe by Hardy because watercress was grown there, obviously provided the writer with just the romantic, rural setting he needed for Jude to be enticed away from his studies.

Continuing in the same direction, take a footpath on the left between a farm and houses. Follow the field edge round left and cross two stiles, ignoring a climbing path on the right. The drive ahead passes the Church of St Michael and All Angels. Twelfth-century, with small Norman arches, it stands in a churchyard that in early February is full of snowdrops.

At the road ahead, turn right passing the Old Rectory again, then climb to take the second footpath on the left; cross a stile and now with a fence on your right retrace your steps to where you left the small copse. Do not enter the woodland but follow the sign ahead through the fields, with the trees on your left and crossing stiles on the way. When the trees end maintain the same line over the open field to reach the Ridgeway. Before leaving the field look back at the view of Wantage, lying in the valley; 'a wide flat low-lying country...under the very verge of his upland world', Jude thought it, when first he saw it.

Turn left along the Ridgeway and soon, on the right, is a hedged path that leads down to Fawley [Marygreen]. If you wish to follow a longer route that Jude often used, turn right on this path to cross 'the great meadow', where he scared birds, and first left into the village. Hardy's grandmother had lived in Fawley in her youth, so family memories may have suggested the location, although, as the writer points out, cottages had been pulled down and trees felled before Jude went to live with Great Aunt Drusilla and Widow Edlin. A footpath leaves Fawley near North Farm and leads to the Wantage Road; here, a mile after turning left, you return to the Courtwood Centre.

On the main walk, continue along the Ridgeway and opposite farm buildings on the right take a path left to an earthwork called Segsbury Castle. Here Arabella came with Jude one evening; he was 'thinking of the great age of the trackway, of the drovers who had frequented it, probably before the Romans knew the country', she was hoping to trap him into marriage when the 'chime of the Church bells signalled that her parents were away from home'.

Return to the Ridgeway and continue in the same direction to reach the road. Just before the junction there are modern cottages on the left, between which, though no trace remains, the Brown House stood; here Jude climbed a ladder to see Oxford. Hardy must have known that it would be difficult to see the town, fifteen or so miles away, with Beacon Hill and the Cumnor Hills hiding it, but maybe it is possible from a high ladder! To finish the walk, turn left and left again, on to the Letcombe Regis Road and find Courthill Centre on the left.

ACKNOWLEDGEMENTS

Extracts from the *Poetical Works of Robert Bridges* (Oxford University Press, 1936) by permission of Oxford University Press.

The estate of Kenneth Grahame – permission for excerpts from the writings of Kenneth Grahame – Curtis Browne Group Ltd.

Excerpts from the poetry of Laurence Binyon by permission of The Society of Authors, on behalf of the Laurence Binyon Estate.

Excerpts from the poetry of John Masefield by permission of The Society of Authors as the literary representative of the Estate of John Masefield.

The estate of DH Lawrence – permission for excerpts from the writings of DH Lawrence – Laurence Pollinger Ltd.

Poetry excerpts from *John Betjeman – Collected Poems* (John Murray, 1966) and *Summoned by Bells* (1960) used by permission of John Murray (Publishers) Ltd.

Permission to quote from the 'Miss Read' books – Penguin UK – Michael Joseph Imprint section.

Permission to quote from the writings of Richard Adams – David Higham Associates Ltd.